A PARISH-BASED APPROACH

HOW TO
Welcome,
Include, AND
Catechize
Children with Autism
and Other Special Needs

LAWRENCE R. SUTTON, PH.D.

LOYOLA PRESS.
A JESUIT MINISTRY
Chicago

LOYOLA PRESS.
A JESUIT MINISTRY

3441 N. Ashland Avenue
Chicago, Illinois 60657
(800) 621-1008
www.loyolapress.com

ISBN-13: 978-0-8294-3890-1
ISBN-10: 0-8294-3890-4
Library of Congress Control Number: 2013948175

Printed in the United States of America.

13 14 15 16 17 18 Versa 10 9 8 7 6 5 4 3 2 1

To my siblings Valerie and David, who were the first to teach me about autism and the importance of spiritual help.

Contents

Preface

". . . catechetical programs should be accessible to persons with disabilities and open to their full, active and conscious participation, according to their capacity."
—*Welcome and Justice for Persons with Disabilities: A Framework of Access and Inclusion*, A Statement of the United States Catholic Bishops

"Let the children come to me."
—Matthew 19:14

Any Catholic who has been paying attention to the Gospels knows that Jesus longs to have everyone at the table. He has come so that we might be one, even as he and the Father are one. And so it's no surprise that the bishops are insistent on achieving the goal of "full, active, and conscious participation" of all young Catholics in religious education programs. This goal flows from the very heart of Christian life and understanding.

Achieving that goal, however, can be a challenge. Each child is unique, and this statement is especially true for children with disabilities. An approach that works for one child may not resonate with another; there is no "one size fits all" lesson or approach. Despite the generous and ingenious efforts of many, the Church has sometimes struggled with effective ways to include children with autism and other cognitive, physical, or developmental disabilities in religious education programs. It's not that we don't know what to do; great strides have been made in public and private schools to serve children with special needs. It's a matter of having the will, the organization, and the resources to meet the challenge of the bishops' words. Sometimes what it takes is a clear pathway to proceed.

Deacon Larry Sutton is doing his part to create such a pathway with his thoughtful and creative approach to providing religious education to the children who are most often overlooked or excluded: children with special needs like autism, Down syndrome, and other cognitive or developmental disabilities.

Sutton saw a challenge and he responded. He was uniquely qualified, blending his roles as both a deacon in the Catholic Church and a psychologist responsible for designing and implementing effective responses to people with autism. His background in these two areas gave Sutton insight into what an effective religious education program for children with special needs would require, and he describes it in this book. To me, reading his story is like watching grace unfold. It's both a manifesto promoting an informed and humane way to provide appropriate religious education for children across a spectrum of special needs and a story of an ordained deacon taking seriously his call to do what deacons do. In other words, he provides a seat at the table for those who are marginalized, poor, imprisoned, sick, or disabled. He sees that no one is forgotten or excluded from the liturgical and communal life of the parish. Sutton acknowledges that the goal of any special needs program is to provide the least restrictive environment for each child and that there are other successful approaches, and he provides us with something fresh, unique, and invigorating for children who might not otherwise be served at all.

In 2012 Loyola Press worked with David and Mercedes Rizzo and their family to publish the *Adaptive First Eucharist Preparation Kit* to help children with special needs and their families prepare for the sacrament. We were gratified to hear the joy expressed by children and their parents at finding this pathway to receive their First Holy Communion. In the process, we became aware of a network of dedicated people who have been working diligently to respond to the needs of children with disabilities. In conversations with those in this ministry, we heard repeatedly, "You should talk to Deacon Larry Sutton. He's got a program that's doing wonders."

So we called Deacon Larry Sutton and visited him at Our Lady of Grace parish in Pittsburgh. There we witnessed a simple, effective program that was serving families of children with autism and other special needs. We saw a program in which dedicated teenagers brought their youthful exuberance, idealism, and creativity to working one-on-one as teen faith mentors. We saw parents gathering to share wisdom, strength, and hope with one another as their children were finally enjoying a parish-based program dedicated to helping each child participate to his or her fullest capacity not only in religious education, but also in parish life. And we saw children learning, praying, singing, and thriving thanks to their connection with a near-peer, a teen faith mentor who was modeling how to know, love, and serve God.

The more we talked with Deacon Larry, the more we knew his story deserved to be told so that others could benefit from what experience has taught him. We hope this book will help parishes that want to be more inclusive in their religious education programs see that it can and has been done successfully.

There are aspects of Deacon Larry's method that stand out and offer a win/win/win/win/win situation. The first is the effective use of teen faith mentors. These are young people who want to do something good, helpful, and even noble. There are plenty of young people who have that desire. With guidance, they have proven to be creative and effective at preparing clever and engaging lessons adapted specifically for the children they have come to know, befriend, and understand. In turn, having one-on-one attention from someone just a bit older than they inspires the children participating in the religious education program. As a result, they are better able to grow in their ability to engage in the lessons, participate in group prayer, and prepare themselves for a lifetime of parish activities.

The parents of the children (who otherwise might not have found a welcoming place in the parish) find joy in their child's religious and spiritual growth, comfort in the care shown their child by the teen faith mentor, and much-needed community as they gather with other parents to share wisdom and support. And the parents of teen faith mentors have the joy of watching their child actively engaged in their faith and growing in conviction as they make a difference in a friend's spiritual journey.

The parish becomes enlivened and transformed as it lives out its mission to be the Body of Christ, welcoming all people to the table of the Lord. In practical terms, Mass attendance and participation in parish life increases as families who have previously felt uncomfortable or unwelcome become engaged in parish life. Likewise, teenagers find new reasons to become involved thanks to their new buddies. In turn, the pastor is empowered to do his good work and guide his flock because they are present and engaged.

Jesus said to his disciples and he says to us, "Let the children come to me." In this book you'll find the actions, inspirations, and guidance you need to fashion your own response to the Lord's command. Take one step at a time, and you'll see grace unfolding for you and for the people of your community.

Introduction

In 2000, a year after I was ordained a deacon, I learned that two second graders with autism, one in my home parish and the other in the parish where I worked, had been denied the Eucharist. The reasons were obscure—I learned about it only after the fact—but the pastoral people involved had concluded that the children's autism somehow barred them from receiving the sacraments. This is contrary to the U.S. bishops' guidelines, which explicitly state that disability in itself never disqualifies a person from the sacraments.

This event offended my sense of social justice. It angered and frustrated me. Here I was—a deacon and a psychologist specializing in autism—unable to bring the sacraments to two children in my own parish. I recalled moments in my deaconate training when our Benedictine teachers challenged us to search for ways to use our gifts in service of God's people. I decided that this was the way God wanted me to serve.

This book is about helping a group of people in your parish experience the grace of the sacraments and the fullness of Catholic life. You probably don't see these people around the parish very often; they tend to keep to themselves. They don't always fit easily into parish programs; they're sometimes ignored and often misunderstood. I'm speaking about Catholics who have the right to be accepted as full members of our Catholic community; to receive the grace of our sacraments; and to worship with us without fear, pity, intimidation, or ridicule. To accomplish this, they need acceptance and some special help—help that you can give with the resources available to you.

This book is specifically about the approach I developed in my parish to provide religious education to children who were not being served. Most parishes have a significant number of these children. They may have autism, Down syndrome, and other disabilities that impair their intellectual, sensory, or social functioning. By definition, these children are different. They are disabled—that is, they lack abilities that other children have. They often aren't enrolled in or might not flourish in typical religious education programs. You might not see them very often because large gatherings—Sunday Mass, for example—can make them anxious. Their presence can make other people anxious, too. In fact, the first step toward bringing these children into an active Catholic life is to make the parish as a whole more receptive to them.

If you are not aware of the needs of these parishioners, you're in good company. I am a clinical psychologist specializing in autism and also an ordained deacon, but I was not aware of the full extent of these children's needs until that event in 2000 opened my eyes.

Searching for a Model

I knew I wanted to help these children receive the sacraments and participate fully in the Church. The question was how. My search for answers brought me into contact with a wonderful group of pastoral leaders and advocates for people with disabilities in the Catholic Church. From these good people, I learned that educating these children is a challenge that all parishes have. I learned, sadly, that while many parishes are making excellent efforts to meet the needs of children with disabilities, the pastoral failure I saw in those two parishes in Pittsburgh is all too common. It's often said that children with disabilities don't need the sacraments because they are "God's special children"—an attitude I find objectionable both as a psychologist and as a cleric. Every Catholic needs the graces of the sacraments. Every child needs to be part of a loving community.

To be sure, fine efforts have been made to form children with autism in the faith. But I knew from my professional work that children with autism often don't thrive in groups or are often bored with material that doesn't challenge them. My

> Every Catholic needs the graces of the sacraments. Every child needs to be part of a loving community.

work has also convinced me that these children are almost always capable of real learning. Often not much is expected from them, so these children aren't given the opportunities they need to learn and express themselves. Some people insist that children with autism be included in regular religious education classes. My professional experience has given me a different perspective on the issue.

Individualized Instruction

Children with autism exhibit a wide range of communication styles, language ability, cognitive ability, and personality. Clinicians refer to it as autism spectrum disorder (ASD) for a good reason. Every child with autism is different. Each is somewhere on a broad spectrum of impairments, ranging from severe to so-called high functioning. As a clinician, I had learned that my first task in helping persons with autism is to get to know them thoroughly. I need to know what they are interested in, what upsets them, what distracts them, how they think, and—most important—how they communicate. Many parishes currently implement some form of individualized religious education plans for children with disabilities, an approach I strongly advocate. There are many different models for religious education. It seems to me that for a program to be effective, it must be adapted to each individual child.

That's the bedrock principle of the method described in this book—the individualized catechesis method. All the instruction is adapted to the individual student, and the teaching is one-on-one. The goal is to prepare these children as well as possible for Reconciliation, Eucharist, and Confirmation, and for adult participation in the Church to the degree to which each child is capable. We can have a curriculum and lesson plans, but how we present the material, and who presents it, is as important as the material itself. Where we present the material is also important—one of the many things we learned since we launched a pilot program at Our Lady of Grace parish in Pittsburgh in 2006.

The pilot program was launched six years after I first heard God's call to work on religious education for children with autism. As I studied the problem and formulated my ideas, a central challenge emerged: where would I find the people who can provide the kind of individualized catechesis that I thought was essential to success? As a professional specializing in autism, I have a healthy respect for professional training and expertise. I've trained professionals. I work with professionals all the time, and I'm keenly aware of the good work that professionals are able to do. But it's also true that people with autism don't live in a strictly professional world. They live with ordinary people who develop relationships with them and come to know them well. Relationship is key.

Perhaps ordinary people with a generous spirit, a liking for others, and an intuitive "feel" for relating to people who are different could be effective teachers for children with autism. If ordinary people could build genuine personal relationships with these children, perhaps as mentors, they could accomplish as much as someone with professional training. Perhaps they could accomplish even more.

Teen Faith Mentors

This idea of ordinary people as mentors led to the most distinctive feature of our program—teen faith mentors. Initially, this was an experiment. I wasn't sure it would work, but I had a good hunch that it might. The hunch was based on my clinical observation of how children and teens with autism learned. I saw that they often responded better to mentors who were close in age to them than they did to adults. A relationship formed more quickly, and the relationship was richer. The results were better. I observed this in both formal and informal settings. I decided to recruit teen mentors for our program.

The experiment worked remarkably well—so well that it's no longer an experiment. This method has been successful, and I'm convinced that the key to its success is the relationship that develops between the student and the teen faith mentor.

Teenagers make good mentors for children with special needs because they come to the job with an open mind. Teenagers don't have fixed ideas about how the children should behave or how much they are capable of learning. I'm convinced that adults consistently sell these children short. Adults often underestimate what these children are capable of, don't ask enough of them, and give in to frustration too quickly. Teenagers don't seem to be as hampered by these attitudes, and thus they are able to build the kind of close relationship that is good for learning.

The dynamics of the situation help make it successful. The teen faith mentors are delighted to work with their own student. They are happy to have a challenge. They want to show what they can do, and they're eager to please the supervising adults and the child's parents. Many children with autism are lonely and isolated, so they are thrilled that a peer or near peer takes an interest in them. The students are eager to please their new friends. This dynamic creates an excellent atmosphere for effective religious education.

Your Parish

Our adaptive religious education program is well established in Our Lady of Grace parish, and I have helped other parishes start programs using this methodology. I've described the method to parishes, to dioceses, and at national conferences. It's been endorsed by influential bishops and by national organizations concerned with the catechesis of Catholics with disabilities, and it is used in Loyola Press's *Adaptive Finding God Program*, which I discuss further in the epilogue. It works. And I'm convinced it can work in your parish, too, with the resources you already have or ones that are readily available to you.

I don't want to give the impression that this is easy. It's not. The method described in this book calls for setting up a new program with all the administrative tasks that a new program entails. Key staff will need to gain an understanding of special needs. You will have to recruit and train new mentors—teenagers who don't fit the conventional catechist profile. You need to learn how to educate children with a variety of abilities and learning styles and who might not fit easily into school settings.

Implementing this program is a commitment. Granted, parishes have many responsibilities, and resources are always limited. But a significant number of children and teens in your parish aren't part of Catholic life, and many are turned away from the sacraments. This is not their choice. They aren't part of things because your parish has yet to provide a way to bring them in. Making the graces of the sacraments available to all Catholics is a moral imperative. Forming the next generation of Catholics in the faith is one of the most important responsibilities of the parish. These responsibilities are not truly fulfilled until they include Catholics with disabilities.

This book describes a way to bring these people in. The first three chapters give a rationale for the program, an overview of autism spectrum disorder, and a description of an individualized catechesis method. The following three chapters are a how-to primer: a description of the roles in the program, how to start a program, and how to support its ongoing life. There's a chapter on sacraments and a chapter highlighting some of the surprises I encountered along the way. Finally, I describe how I have partnered with Loyola Press to build a curriculum using individualized catechesis and adaptive materials, which will make a religious education program for children with autism and other special needs a possibility for all parishes.

We are called to serve—as St. Lawrence, the deacon of Rome, referred to persons with disabilities—the treasures of our Church. All Catholics have a place in our community, at God's altar. The time is now, with the leadership of Pope Francis, to serve and include all of God's people. Godspeed.

Unable to get near Jesus because of the crowd, they opened up the roof above him.

—Mark 2:4

1

Religious Education and Children with Disabilities

Jesus loved children. A passage much beloved by religious educators is Matthew 18:1–5, in which Jesus calls a child to him and tells the onlookers, "Unless you turn and become like children, you will not enter the kingdom of heaven." He continues, "And whoever receives one child such as this in my name receives me." Jesus showed great compassion to people on the fringes of society, including people with disabilities: lepers, and those who were blind, deaf, and mute. When you hold a banquet, he said, don't invite your friends and rich neighbors, but "invite the poor, the crippled, the lame, the blind" (Luke 14:13).

Jesus' words and example challenge everyone in the Church, particularly pastoral leaders of our parishes and dioceses. Everybody belongs in the Church, especially those who are poor or afflicted and others who may not fit our expectations of who belongs alongside us in our pews. It's not always easy to make room for people with disabilities. By definition, they are different: disabled, which means that they lack abilities that most others have. We must reach out, listen, make accommodations, and take extra steps even when those steps take us down unfamiliar pathways.

Nowhere is this challenge greater than in religious education. In most parishes, religious education—formal and informal—takes more time, effort, and resources than anything else the parish does. And rightly so; nothing is more essential.

Too often, children with disabilities are not fully included in this process, and many aren't part of it at all. Many parents assume that their children can't be part of a program designed for "normally abled" children. Many are afraid that others in the parish won't receive their children well. Many parents are afraid that their children will fail. Children with disabilities like autism often struggle in normal religious education programs. The typical techniques of explanation, discussion, and participation in group projects don't suit their learning styles. Most catechists lack the training to adapt materials for children with sensory-processing difficulties, underdeveloped social skills, and other impairments.

It's a challenge to form children with these types of disabilities in the faith, but it's a challenge that we're fully capable of meeting. The skill of teaching is the ability to present material effectively to children who learn at different speeds and in different ways. Children with autism spectrum disorder simply stretch these skills further than usual. Most of these children can learn the most important ideas and tenets of the Catholic faith. They can learn more than we think they can. What's needed are tools and a strategy to extend the skills that religious educators already have to include children who don't learn the way most children do.

This book presents an approach to the religious education for children with autism and other special needs. This program works. The average parish, or a cluster of parishes, can make it work with the resources already available in the local faith community. And the *Adaptive Finding God Program* makes it even more achievable by providing materials that break down the *Catechism of the Catholic Church* into simple, concrete lessons, using learning tools and activities for different levels and learning styles.

Before we explain the approach, let's consider what the Church has said about the religious education of Catholics with disabilities.

What the Church Says

The Church has spoken in several important documents about the pastoral needs of Catholics with disabilities. In 1978, the U.S. Conference of Catholic Bishops (USCCB) issued the *Pastoral Statement on Persons with Disabilities*, and in 1995, it published *Guidelines for the Celebration of the Sacraments with Persons with Disabilities*. Catechetical issues were discussed in *General Directory for Catechesis*, published by the Vatican in 1997, and in *National Directory for Catechesis*, published by the USCCB in 2005. The following sections summarize the main points of these documents.

People with Disabilities Are Full Members of the Church

The 1978 *Pastoral Statement* puts it this way: "Persons with disabilities . . . seek to serve the community and to enjoy their full baptismal rights as members of the Church" (no. 33).

This is the central principle we must keep in mind when thinking about Catholics with disabilities. Every baptized Catholic is fully part of the Church. This point sounds self-evident, but it's really not. We often ascribe special statuses or categories to various Catholics, but doing so has its risks. Catholics with disabilities have sometimes been put into a category of "special people," set apart from others. The *Pastoral Statement* reminds us that people with disabilities have the same identity and the same right to participate fully in the life of the Church as everyone else.

The Church Isn't Fully Itself Unless People with Disabilities Participate Fully in Its Life

According to the 1978 *Pastoral Statement*, "The Church finds its true identity when it fully integrates itself with [persons with disabilities]" (no. 12).

This point flows directly from the principle that people with disabilities are full members of the Church. The word *catholic* means "universal." The community of faith is impoverished when people with disabilities (or any others) are

> The community of faith is impoverished when people with disabilities (or any others) are excluded from it or fail to fully participate in it.

excluded from it or fail to fully participate in it. We are less than we should be. This gives the principle of inclusion a certain transcendent importance. The Church is not inclusive in any contingent sense, when it is merely convenient, affordable, or easy. By its very nature, the Church includes everyone to the fullest extent possible.

People with Disabilities Have Something to Offer

The USCCB's Guidelines for the "Celebration of the Sacraments with Persons with Disabilities" state, "By reason of their baptism, all Catholics are equal in dignity in the sight of God and have the same divine calling." The *National Directory for Catechesis* says of people with disabilities: "Their involvement enriches every aspect of Church life. They are not just the recipients of catechesis—they are also its agents" (no. 49).

All Catholics, including Catholics with disabilities, are capable of proclaiming the Gospel and witnessing to the truth of the Salvation that comes through Christ. People with disabilities make the Church the inclusive, universal community it is meant to be. Through their love, generosity, and patient endurance, they carry out the virtues that all Christians hope for.

The Parish Is Where Inclusion Happens

According to the 1978 *Pastoral Statement*, "The parish is the door to participation for persons with disabilities, and it is the responsibility of the pastor and lay leaders to make sure that this door is always open" (no. 18).

As much as possible, Catholics with disabilities live their lives as Catholics in parishes, not in special programs operated away from their parish community. The parish is where they worship, serve, and receive their religious education. The responsibility for ensuring that they are served well falls squarely on parish leadership. Thankfully, many parishioners often have skills, interest, or latent talents and can help meet this responsibility in caring and creative ways.

Programs and Services Must Fit the Particular Abilities and Circumstances of People with Disabilities

The *General Directory for Catechesis* urges that "personalized and adequate programs" be developed for persons with disabilities (no. 189).

To make catechesis effective, educators must adapt existing materials, develop new materials and methods, and embrace new classroom approaches. That means that they must understand each individual child's disability well enough to design and adopt effective teaching strategies. This book is intended to help catechetical leaders do this.

There Are No Excuses

Pope John Paul II wrote in the apostolic exhortation *Catechesi Tradendae* (*On Catechesis in Our Time*) that children with disabilities "have a right, like others of their age, to know the mystery of faith" (no. 41). The *National Directory for Catechesis* says that "the Church owes persons with disabilities her best efforts in order to ensure that they are able to hear the Gospel of Christ, receive the Sacraments, and grow in their faith in the fullest and richest manner possible" (no. 49).

The parish must provide people with disabilities with meaningful access to catechesis and to the sacraments. It's a matter of justice. It's a matter of being who we are meant to be: the Body of Christ.

Children with Disabilities in the Parish

Children with disabilities need to be incorporated into the parish as all parishioners are. Pastors and catechetical leaders need to reach out to them, understand their disabilities, and meet each individual child's needs. In many cases, parish educators will need to find and identify these children. Their parents may be apprehensive about how the parish will receive their children and whether the parish can accommodate their special needs. Indeed, one of the biggest tasks is to educate the parish as a whole about the needs of parishioners with disabilities. The following sections present some of the tasks that parish ministers need to accomplish.

Understand Disabilities—and Abilities

Ministry to children with disabilities begins with understanding. You don't need to become an expert, but you do need to know enough about the child's disability to determine what the child needs and how to meet those needs.

The best source of information is usually the child's parents. Parents know their child better than anyone else, and many of them have acquired considerable knowledge about their child's particular disability. You might also draw on the expertise of professionals in the field of special education. Some may even be members of your parish. At the same time, it's important not to label children or stereotype them. A good approach is to focus on what the child *can* do and then build on the child's strengths. It's especially important to understand how the child communicates and how he or she learns best.

Sometimes this task is relatively straightforward; sometimes it's quite difficult. The problem is that children with autism often cannot communicate easily, making it difficult to assess their abilities. George, a young man with autism, illustrates some of these challenges. When he was entering kindergarten, George scored a 64 on a standard IQ test, a score that placed him in the range of mild intellectual disability. Ten years later, in high school, George scored a 72, placing him in the borderline range of normal intellectual functioning. When he was twenty-one years old, a government vocational agency administered a third IQ test; this time George's score was 94, a result that put him in the average range of intelligence. Each time, the psychologist administering the test certified the results as accurate. It's widely thought that a person's IQ is a measurement of an innate ability that doesn't change over a lifetime. Why, then, did George's IQ score change so substantially?

I think George had average intelligence all along. Autism is a condition that affects a person's ability to process information through language and sensory data. When he was young, George didn't have the language, processing ability, and/or confidence to express his actual intellectual abilities. Over time, George got better at taking tests and learned how to compensate for impaired processing ability. It's often difficult to determine what a child with autism knows. George's case illustrates why it is best to avoid labels and instead design an instructional approach that fits the abilities of each individual.

Build Relationships

Relationships are the heart of catechesis. The point of catechesis is to help people have a relationship with God. We accomplish this in large part through the relationships that we build with others in the parish. Specifically, the relationships that teen faith mentors develop with the children they teach and the children's parents are the key to providing individualized religious education.

Building relationships isn't always easy. Parish ministers must deal with barriers to good relationships. Communication can be difficult. Most children with ASD cannot process information as quickly as other children can. It takes them longer to understand what you are saying. It takes them longer to respond to you. Sometimes the delayed response can be painfully long—up to a minute or more. Don't be upset by this. Sometimes children might appear to be resisting you and acting out on purpose. Usually they are not; they cannot process information like others typically can.

Learning styles among children with ASD are varied. Because they have trouble with language, children with autism and some other disabilities often learn better when material is presented visually or in the form of a story. They like structure, routine, and predictability. When instructing these children in catechesis, it is important to prepare them by anticipating things that might produce anxiety for them and by repeating and making Catholic prayers and catechetical concepts visual.

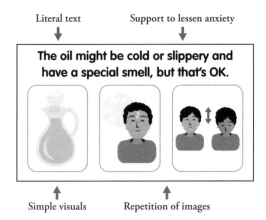

Most children tend to be self-centered; children with ASD show this trait in abundance. They often appear very egocentric, taking little account of others' needs. This is not a moral failing; rather, it is an impairment that is directly attributable to the disability itself. Children with autism often have great difficulty understanding that other people have minds of their own, and this often manifests in times of stress. For example, a young man with autism might experience his mother's death as a personal assault against him and be unaware that his father and siblings are also experiencing profound grief. He might blame the doctor or God or perhaps the pastor of his parish.

Children with ASD often do not make eye contact. This is because they don't understand emotions and are unsettled by the feelings they see in another person's eyes. Don't be offended when children don't look at you or acknowledge you when you speak to them. It's not personal; it's a characteristic of the disability.

Parish ministers need to take these issues into account when building relationships. Remember that delayed responses, language problems, self-centeredness, and other traits are the consequences of a developmental disorder. They are not character defects that can be corrected or habits a child can break if he or she tries hard enough. Autism spectrum disorders are lifelong and permanent. Their social and intellectual consequences can often be managed to some degree, but they cannot be eliminated.

Provide Individualized Catechesis

Children need religious education that suits their individual needs. They might learn differently, or they might relate differently, than other children. In many cases, the nature of their disability puts limits on what they will be able to understand and the degree to which they can participate in ordinary parish life. At the same time, parishioners with disabilities have the same need as everyone else to experience the spiritual riches of the Catholic Church. Like everyone else, they need Mass, the sacraments, and prayer.

The goal is inclusion, but what does inclusion mean for people whose impairments set them apart? The ever-present risk is that we will settle for a kind of partial, grudging inclusion. We've all experienced it. It's being invited to a party where you're not completely welcome. It's joining a group and feeling that you don't really belong, that the other people in the group would be just fine if you weren't there.

This book outlines a model of inclusion for children with disabilities that brings them into Catholic life in a way that maximizes their abilities, builds on their strengths, and compensates for their disabilities. It relies on near-peer-age mentors to provide individualized instruction and employs a variety of creative techniques and materials to communicate the concepts of faith and the sacraments in ways suitable for children with various impairments. In this way, they grow into Catholic life as deeply as they are able and are included as fully as they are able when they are confirmed.

Educate the Parish

One of the most important challenges facing parish leaders is the task of educating the parish. Some parishioners are disturbed by people with disabilities, or they see them as "different." Some children with

ASD cope with anxiety and sensory overload by self-stimulatory behavior, known as "stimming"—flapping their hands, bouncing up and down, making noises. Many are socially impaired. They don't make eye contact, read social cues, or respond well to questions or instructions. Their presence can make Sunday Mass a livelier occasion than many parishioners like.

A common reaction is that parishioners avoid children with ASD or other disabilities. People with disabilities often aren't invited into visible roles of service. Their needs aren't considered when planning parish events. Too often, people with disabilities aren't seen at all. Parents might keep their children with disabilities away from Mass and out of religious education, fearing that they will not be welcomed or understood. When this happens, the entire community is diminished.

Parish leaders need to make a concerted effort to make the parish a more welcoming, inclusive community. Parishioners with disabilities—children and adults—need to be welcomed into full participation. Their presence needs to be acknowledged openly, from the pulpit and in other public forums. The parish needs to seek them out, greet them gladly, and make whatever accommodations are necessary.

The second chapter of the Gospel of Mark recounts the story of Jesus healing a paralytic man. Four of the man's friends had carried him on a pallet to Jesus' house. Finding the house too crowded, the men cut a hole in the roof and lowered their friend into Jesus' presence. The four men went to great lengths to bring their friend to Jesus. We need to be like them: willing to do whatever is necessary to bring our brothers and sisters with disabilities into the life of our parishes. We need to creatively find ways to bring them to receive Christ's healing love.

Getting to Know Nick

The story of Nick illustrates many of the tasks and challenges I've been discussing. Nick is a twelve-year-old boy with cerebral palsy who gets around with the help of a walker. He has significant hearing loss, and because his fine motor control is impaired, it is difficult for him to swallow food. Nick can read, but most of the time he can't speak clearly enough to be understood. Instead, he uses a communications device to talk to others.

When Nick came for religious education, the first step was to meet with his parents to understand his condition and to ask what they wanted the parish to do for their son. Did they want him to receive full religious education, or did they just want him to be able to come to Mass? Did they want us to prepare him to receive sacraments? Did they want him to receive private one-on-one instruction, or did they want him to be part of a larger religious education class? It's very important to listen carefully to parents and, if possible, to the child, too. The first question is, "What do you want?"

Nick's parents were apprehensive. They wanted their son to receive as full a religious education as possible, but they were uneasy about how he would be received. Nick's fine motor impairment made it hard for him to control saliva. He was constantly wiping his mouth, and sometimes he drooled. On several occasions, people had reacted to this with repugnance. This worried and offended his parents, and because of this they didn't bring him to Mass very often.

Nick joined the religious education class, but much of his class time was spent with a sixteen-year-old girl who had been trained as a faith mentor for children with disabilities. Nick related more easily to a near peer than to an adult, which is something that I've found is typical of children with disabilities—indeed, with most children. Nick began coming to Mass regularly. He used a hearing aid and followed along with the help of a detailed guide to the Mass. We talked to Nick's parents and physician about how he should receive the Eucharist, and it was decided that he would receive it under the form of the Precious Blood only.

Nick became more a part of the parish. His disability is out there for everyone to see; he uses a walker, he has trouble speaking clearly, and sometimes he drools. But he is outwardly friendly and easy to like, and people who spend time with Nick like him a lot.

We are a better parish because Nick is part of it.

2

Autism and Other Special Needs

While my expertise and professional experience is with autism spectrum disorder, the program I started at my parish has been successful for children with other disabilities as well. Disabilities come in many forms and degrees of severity. These are some of the students recently enrolled in our program:

Anne, nine years old, has very limited vision. She cannot see much of what is happening on the altar during Mass. She can read some material using a special device.

Nick, twelve, has cerebral palsy. He has significant hearing loss and is not able to talk. He gets around with the aid of a walker.

Josh, ten, has a high-functioning form of autism. His interactions with teachers and peers are a struggle for him, and he is easily distracted in new settings. He doesn't pay close attention in class, but he has above-average intelligence.

Denise, nine years old, has severe autism. She does not speak. It's difficult to know what she understands, and she frequently becomes agitated in church and class.

Mark, age ten, has Down syndrome. His intellectual capacity is limited. He has a sweet disposition. Everybody loves Mark.

All of these children benefit from individualized instruction. The first step is to understand their disabilities.

These impairments associated with disabilities can affect people's ability to take care of themselves, to communicate, to learn, to get around, and to live independently. Some impairments are sensory; they involve vision or hearing loss. Some are physical and can affect the ability to walk, fine motor control, and coordination and movement. Others are neurological, including autism, epilepsy, and other seizure disorders. In many cases, disabilities impair intellectual functioning.

Autism

The disability with which I am most familiar and one frequently seen by religious educators is autism spectrum disorder. *Spectrum* refers to the fact that people's impairments range from relatively mild to severe. Autism disorders are diagnosed by observing a child's behavior and development in early childhood. Autism is a lifelong disorder that can't be cured, but if correctly diagnosed, it can be successfully managed. There are currently no blood tests or genetic screenings for ASD. Autism is not a mental illness or a psychiatric disorder. Children with autism don't as a rule need medication, psychotherapy, or psychiatric treatment. They need help managing their lives.

Every person with autism is different, but there are some common traits of people with ASD. Many of these things are illustrated by the case of Anthony, a young man whom I first got to know professionally as a psychologist and later in our adaptive religious education program. Anthony's early development did not progress within the norm. He didn't respond to verbal cues very well, and he didn't seem to look at his mother very much. He didn't talk. It took Anthony's parents a while to realize that something wasn't right. Anthony was their first child; like many new parents, they didn't have much contact with other children to provide a comparison. They took him to an audiologist when he was about two years old, but he didn't seem to have a hearing problem. Then they took him to a speech and language pathologist. Soon after, Anthony was diagnosed with autism. He didn't say more than a word or two at a time until he was nine years old. He would express his frustration at not being understood by banging his head on the desk and screaming. Sometimes he would strike his face with a closed fist. He didn't respond normally to pain.

When language finally came to Anthony, he responded very slowly. His parents, a teacher, or another child would ask a question, but it took Anthony a long time to answer—sometimes as long as ninety seconds. When the answer finally came, it was usually correct, but often the other person, frustrated by waiting, wasn't around to hear it. With his language impairment, Anthony couldn't take a standard IQ test. His teachers thought his intelligence was low, and they tried to steer him into a life-skills curriculum to learn basic skills. His parents insisted that he receive normal school instruction.

Anthony came to our religious education program when he was fourteen years old. His faith mentor was Lily, a high school freshman. In an early class, Lily mentioned the idea of sin, and Anthony asked, "Do you mean like Cain and Abel?" He proceeded in a slow and methodical way to tell the story of Cain and Abel from the Old Testament. Anthony's father and I witnessed this; we were both astonished. I had been Anthony's psychologist for five years; this was the first time I had heard him say more than a few words at a time. His father had no idea how Anthony knew the story of Cain and Abel. Neither he nor Anthony's mother had told him the story. None of us had any idea how a boy who was thought to have a significant intellectual disability could pull the story out of thin air as soon as his mentor mentioned the concept of sin.

This illustrates something that I will say often in this book: people with autism are usually unable to understand what's going on in other people's minds, but the reverse is also true. We don't know what's going on in the minds of people with autism. Anthony reminded me how important it is, in my interactions with people with autism, to complete my thoughts and explain things clearly, even if the person doesn't give me any feedback or even seem to be listening. People with autism often know much more than you think.

Anthony was confirmed at age twenty. He learned about the Gifts of the Holy Spirit and is able to explain them. He says common prayers and can participate in some small-group activities, although he prefers to spend time by himself. He goes to Mass and appears to understand it. He receives the Eucharist regularly. Anthony is an active, involved member of his parish.

What Autism Is

Autism is a disorder of the brain's ability to process information. Sensory data gets jumbled. Language ability is impaired. People with autism can't make sense of the verbal and nonverbal cues, hints, body language, and emotions that make up the subtle web of social interaction in which we all live. The cause of autism is unknown. It may be caused by genetic mutations. It may be caused by combinations of normal genes. It may be a condition with some genetic basis that is triggered by environmental factors. We just don't know. But it's not rare. According to the March 2013 Center for Disease Control National Health Statistics Report, about one in every fifty children is affected by autism. Autism is four times more prevalent in boys than girls.

Autism is a developmental disability that manifests itself in early childhood, and it is diagnosed through the observation of poor social skills, limited communication, repetitive behaviors, and a limited range of interests and activities.

Social Skills Without direction or teaching, children and adults with autism typically show a low ability to respond to family members and a limited ability to interact with others. They often don't know or understand how to engage in simple social interactions.

Children with autism typically play alone. They don't know how to start or sometimes how to continue conversations while playing. They often can't anticipate or draw logical, parallel conclusions or deductions because of deficits in executive functioning. They often lack the ability to connect past experience with present action or to plan and organize. As a consequence, they rarely have success in reaching out to others.

Communication Skills Delayed and impaired language development is another characteristic of autism. Some people with autism never develop functional language. Many have quite limited vocabularies. Even those capable of complex speech show abnormalities such as echolalia (repeating words spoken by others), unconventional word use, and unusual inflection. As noted earlier, people with autism typically have difficulty with nonverbal communication such as eye contact; body language; and reading facial, nonverbal, and social cues.

Rigid and Restricted Behavior People with autism typically have narrow and unusual interests. For example, my friend Anthony reads obsessively about the Revolutionary War. He can recite precise details about battles and the names of officers. Many follow rigid routines and can become quite upset when these routines are disrupted. Many, particularly as children, have numerous sensory problems; for instance, they are picky eaters because of a food's texture or smell; they are bothered by materials, tags, and seams in clothing; and they are highly sensitive to noise.

Stimming People with autism often engage in "stimming." Typical stims are hand flapping, bouncing up and down, rocking back and forth, and making noise. Stimming often functions as communication; that is a way to express frustration, happiness, and excitement. It is also a reaction to stress. Children with autism are often hypersensitive to sights and sounds, and their ability to process sensory data is faulty. So they relieve the anxiety and confusion they feel or express themselves by stimming.

Autism is a developmental disorder. The key word is *disorder*: the development of people with autism is out of order; it is not uniformly impaired. For example, a child with Down syndrome might have the developmental functioning of a six-year-old across all skill areas—social, language, behavioral—and that level of functioning will persist throughout his or her life. A person with autism can have low function in some areas and average or even above-average functioning in others. About 2 percent of people with autism have remarkable savant-like abilities. For example, a child with autism might not be able to carry on a simple conversation but can name the players on the rosters of all thirty teams in Major League Baseball or perform complex mathematical calculations rapidly without use of paper or a calculator.

Autism is	Autism is NOT
A disorder of the brain's ability to process information	A psychiatric disorder or mental illness
A developmental disability that affects social, behavioral, and communication skills	A phase that will pass
A disorder that causes variable functioning. People with autism are not uniformly impaired	A result of child-rearing, stress in the home, or evil spirits, God's punishment

This varied functioning is the reason for much heartache and frustration for parents and others who interact with people with autism. They may think, "If he can talk about cars in such detail, why doesn't he talk to me when I ask a question? If he can multiply five-digit numbers in his head, why doesn't he respond when his mother hugs him?" But people with autism cannot do these things. Their disability is developmental. Something is lacking that cannot be supplied; they have to learn these skills that you and I have instinctually. People with autism can learn to compensate for their impairments, often by carefully following scripted behaviors, but this requires intervention.

What Autism Is Not

It's important to be clear about what autism is not. It is not considered a psychiatric disorder or a mental illness. These things are clinically significant patterns or syndromes rooted in an individual's life situation, brain chemistry, or other causes. The symptoms of psychiatric disorders usually change over time. They can usually be treated. By contrast, autism is a developmental disorder that is lifelong and relatively static.

Autism is not a phase that will pass. The neurological impairments present at birth will always be present. They will manifest differently as a person grows older, and they can often be managed, but they will not change substantially. Teachers can help people with autism work around and manage some of these impairments, but they can't help them "get better." Even those who are very bright may return to stimming in times of sickness, grief, or severe stress.

Autism is not caused by deficient child rearing, stress in the home, or other psychological factors in the child's environment. It is not caused by evil spirits. It is not God's punishment for parents' sins. Autism can occur in any family. The condition is found in all societies and in all racial and ethnic groups.

For people with ASD, stimming and other unusual behaviors associated with autism are not intentional. They are not hostile acts meant to disrupt groups or stratagems to get out of class. They are forms of communication or reactions to excitement, stress, and confusion caused by the faulty processing of sensory input. There's nothing about it that we should take personally.

Theory of Mind and Executive Functioning

Two concepts from psychology—theory of mind and executive functioning—help us to better understand people with autism. Theory of mind is the ability to understand that other people have beliefs, desires, attitudes, and feelings that are different from one's own. It's called a theory because the mind isn't directly observable. Each of us has an intuitive understanding that we have a mind; in normal development, children soon develop a theory that other people have minds, too. This theory is shown to be valid every time we discern what someone else is thinking or feeling and are shown to be correct. Theory of mind is the basis for empathy. We cannot have intimate relationships without it.

Theory-of-mind abilities are typically impaired in people with autism. They have difficulty grasping that others think differently than they do. They don't understand that the things that happen to them happen to other people, too, and that other people are happy, sad, frustrated, and excited as a result of those things. This impairment is the source of the self-centeredness often observed in people with autism. They are quite literally stuck with themselves.

Thus, people with autism assume that everyone else shares their experiences. They feel that they don't have to explain anything because they assume that we know exactly what they are thinking. (What else would we be thinking?) A man doesn't have to explain why he is late for work because his boss already knows why. A child won't tell her mother why she is angry because her mother already knows. A boy assumes that everyone is as interested as he is in the rosters of Major League Baseball teams and the details of Revolutionary War battles.

We "mind read" all the time. We read faces, pick up cues from body language, and attend to nuances of tone when other people are speaking. We judge when it's appropriate to smile, frown, laugh, and speak. Imagine what life is like for someone who can't do this. They might talk endlessly about their favorite topic long past the point at which a polite listener has communicated in a dozen nonverbal ways that it's time to move on to something else. They might laugh at a funeral, fail to say thank you for gifts, or get angry when they are called for dinner.

Autism and Theory of Mind	
Individuals with autism often struggle to take another's perspective or "put themselves in another's shoes"	How Catechists, Teachers, and Others Can Help
Difficulty explaining their own behavior	Teach the concepts of emotions and feelings.
Difficulty understanding emotions	Teach awareness that others have their own state of mind.
Difficulty predicting others' behaviors or emotional states	Teach how to read nonverbal and social cues.
Problems understanding perspectives of others	Review different perspectives.
Problems inferring the intentions of others	Practice social situations.
Lack of understanding that behavior impacts how others think and feel	Role-play/rehearse.
Problems with joint attention and other social conventions	Engage in collaborative, sensory-friendly games or activities.
Problems differentiating fact from fiction	Support abstract concepts with scripts and visual aids.

Social life is chaotic and painful for people with theory-of-mind deficits, so they learn coping strategies. One strategy is to adhere to rules and routines. When you don't know what's expected of you, clinging to an established routine makes life more predictable and less surprising. People with autism often develop highly detailed rules and become very upset when they are asked to alter them. Another coping strategy is to imitate what others do in social situations. This helps, but because the person doesn't understand the nuances of social behavior, imitation is a partial solution at best. I observed an embarrassing example at a Baptism where I presided. After the ceremony, a young man with autism watched carefully as family members came up to the mother and greeted her with hugs and kisses. The man was not part of the woman's family and had never met her. Nevertheless, he approached the woman and tried to kiss and hug her; he was shocked when she pushed him away. He had made a mistake in guessing that hugging and kissing is "what you do" at Baptisms.

Unable to recognize linguistic nuance, people with autism tend to take words literally and believe everything they are told. This tendency, combined with blindness to social cues, can cause social disasters. A person with autism might ask an overweight woman why she is so fat or a bald man why his head is shiny. They often do not get jokes or understand lying and deceit. This can have difficult results. I have worked with autistic young people in a juvenile prison in Pennsylvania. A number of them had done exactly what their "friend" told them to do, having no idea that it was illegal until the police arrested them.

Another disability, one that can be even more troubling, is impairment of what psychologists call executive functioning. This is the ability to manage cognitive processes such as memory, attention, problem solving, reasoning, and language and use that information to manage the future. All these processes must work together if a person is to learn, communicate, and work. Executive functioning allows us to think abstractly. It's the ability to be flexible and adapt to changing conditions.

For many people with autism, this management is jumbled and disorderly. They have difficulty understanding cause and effect, that something they do now will have an impact on later events. That makes it very difficult to make any kind of plan. They have difficulty generalizing; they experience every situation as novel. A child might see that two plus two equals four, but not that four can also be obtained by adding one and three or four and zero. This impairment makes relationships difficult. An autistic boy with a crush on a classmate might not be deterred when she tells him to go away. Every day is a new day. He might approach her again and again, not understanding that a firm rebuff means that she's really not interested in him.

The Autism Spectrum

In describing the manifestations of autism, I've used many qualifying words such as *frequently, often, sometimes,* and

> Assume nothing, and build on strengths.

might. That's because it's hard to generalize about the symptoms of autism. Autism is diagnosed by observing behavior, but the observed behavior varies tremendously from person to person. I've worked with thousands of people with autism. No two are alike. Thus, we have something of a paradox. The disabilities of autism are permanent, but in almost all cases, the weaknesses are accompanied by strengths. A child's intellectual abilities may be low, but she may have relatively strong language. A boy might have fairly good social skills but also engage in severe stimming. It's important to carefully observe children with autism. Assume nothing, and build on strengths.

Psychologists account for the variability of symptoms by speaking of autism spectrum disorders. At one end of the spectrum is what used to be referred to as Asperger syndrome, a high-functioning form of autism. Children with this condition do not have problems with early language development and do not show the cognitive deficits that other people with autism have. They do show the other problems associated with autism: poor social skills, repetitive behavior, an attachment to routines and rituals, and subtle problems such as avoidance of eye contact and odd gestures. Many higher-functioning children aren't diagnosed for many years because their language and intellectual development are typical.

Pastoral Care of People with Autism

Pastoral care of people with autism begins by making the parish a comfortable, welcoming place. Many parents of children with autism are reluctant to bring their children to Mass or religious education. They worry about how their children will cope with an unfamiliar muddle of sights and sounds and with contact with new people. They fear that their children's stimming will upset other parishioners. Pastoral ministers need to seek out these children and their families and assure them that they will be welcome.

Of course, pastoral ministers need to follow through on that promise. In my parish, we make people with autism visible. A man with autism in his forties serves as an usher. Each week it's his responsibility to fill the holy water fonts, help with the weekly collections, and bring the food basket to the altar at Mass. A man with severe hearing loss is a lector. A woman with Down syndrome serves at weekday masses. Teens with autism serve as teachers and aides in my religious education program. Visibility builds familiarity. When people see an usher with autism, other people with ASD feel comfortable at Mass, and it gets easier to invite them to participate in other parish activities. This is great.

I encourage clergy to talk about autism and other disabilities from the pulpit. I have done this in many parishes, and I have found it to be a highly effective way to open the door. It's helpful to demystify the disabilities and their associated behaviors. This fosters a people-first attitude where we see a person who happens to have a disability rather than a disabled person. When I talk about autism in parishes for the first time, I make it a point to go directly to stimming—the core concern for many in the pews. I explain that things like noises, hand flapping, and bouncing are behavioral responses to what people with autism are seeing and hearing. I point to the stained-glass windows, gleaming on a sunny Sunday morning. I mention the sounds of the organ, the flickering candles, and the colorful vestments and ask people how they would feel if they didn't have words to describe the emotions these things aroused in them. That's the predicament of people with autism: they can't express happiness and excitement (or anxiety and boredom) in words, so they use actions.

It's a truism that there is no substitute for personal, individual attention when it comes to pastoral care. This is certainly true for parish ministers relating to people with autism. Individual attention is the cornerstone of the religious education program that's described in this book. It needs to be the foundation of other pastoral initiatives as well.

A story will illustrate the point. I discovered that a young mother of two boys with autism did not come to Mass because her sons couldn't sit through it. They reacted to the sights and sounds of Mass with severe stimming. Over eighteen months, I worked with the mother to accustom her sons to Mass in a process of gradual familiarization.

We started by walking around the church before Mass began. The boys, who were extremely attuned and sensitive to sounds, plucked on the piano keys. One of them played short melodies. For weeks, the mother and her sons sat in the back of church and stayed a little longer for each Mass. At first they heard the opening announcements and left before Mass began. Then they stayed through the opening hymn, then the Liturgy of the Word. It took four months for the boys to be able to stay through the reading of the Gospel. The homily was difficult for them to get through. The boys like predictability and routine, and homilies are hard to predict. Some homilies are long, some are short, some are interesting, and some are dull. It took several more months for the boys to be able to get through the homily comfortably.

We proceeded through the Mass at a steady pace week after week. The boys were being prepared to receive the Eucharist, and they were eager to see this part of the Mass "for real." In class they practiced receiving the unconsecrated host. Often their teen mentors would sit with them at Mass. It took nearly eighteen months for the boys to be able to attend an entire Mass from opening announcements to closing hymn. They don't just sit through it; they participate. They receive the Eucharist, they pray, they understand what is happening on the altar. The boys (and their mother) are participating in the life of our parish to the extent that they are able. That's what good pastoral care can and should accomplish.

3

The Individualized Catechesis Method

Most parishes in the United States operate a religious education program, and many of them accommodate children with developmental and physical disabilities. Many parishes use an individual religious education plan or something like it to note the learning strengths and needs of the student and to develop adaptations to suit the needs of individual students. Thankfully, individualized plans are becoming more and more common. Sometimes children with disabilities are "mainstreamed," or placed in regular classes, because they don't require any special adaptations.

Nevertheless, children with autism and some other developmental disabilities do have special needs, and parishes using the mainstreaming model take various measures to accommodate these children. Some programs leave it up to the catechist-teacher to overcome the barriers to learning. Sometimes parents, tutors, catechists, or other support staff will sit with the child in class to give whatever assistance is necessary. Some programs supplement the mainstreaming approach with special services. Children might receive special tutoring outside of class, or they might split their time between the regular class and special instruction in another room.

Some parishes have special classes that supplement their main-streamed class, where children with disabilities come together and learn about God as a community. In this way, they are exposed to their peers but also receive some form of specialized instruction.

The individualized catechesis method that I have developed provides an alternative approach. In it, the children are not mainstreamed until they are confirmed. Neither are they put in a special group of their own. Instead, each child is taught individually by a near-peer mentor in an environment suited for children with sensory-processing impairments and intellectual deficits. This method has proved highly effective in preparing children for the sacraments and teaching them the basic tenets of our faith. In my experience, children with autism learn more effectively with this method of instruction.

The Program in a Nutshell

Our parish program features one-on-one instruction provided by volunteer teen mentors, who are supervised by a catechist, program coordinator, or catechetical leader. These mentors are teenagers from the parish who have been trained to work with children with autism and other special needs. The children and teen mentors are carefully matched, and almost all the instruction is personal, one-on-one work between them, which enhances communication and attention. This approach also involves customizing materials and strategies to particular learning and communication styles.

Students and teen mentors work in rooms that have been arranged to minimize distractions. The lighting is low and indirect. The decor is simple. Furniture, globes, plants, and other educational material in the classrooms are put aside as much as possible. Every effort is made to shield the room from outside noise. Teen faith mentors and their students work in a quiet and sensory-benign environment.

The teen mentors work from lesson plans that have been developed by the program coordinator and/or catechetical leader to meet the needs of children with developmental and intellectual disabilities. Teaching emphasizes narrative stories and visual learning. The curriculum covers core material in a religious education program, including sacramental preparation for the Eucharist, Reconciliation, and Confirmation. When a child enters the program, catechists, teen mentors, and program staff work closely with the child's parents to develop a course of study that fits the child's capacities and abilities. Each child works toward this goal at his or her own pace. The overall goal is to see that each child is confirmed as an adult member of the Catholic Church and is welcomed and encouraged to participate in the life of the Church to the best of his or her individual ability.

An important feature of the program is parents' participation. Parents work closely with teen mentors, as parents usually know their child's abilities and learning style better than anyone else does. Mentors review each lesson with the parents, and parents are expected to repeat the lesson at least once at home. During class, the parents sit together for a facilitated discussion; at our parish the volunteer facilitator has experience working with families affected by autism.

Children with autism typically need structure and routine to focus their attention. At the beginning of each year, a consistent routine for class time is established. We begin together with a song (usually one of the parents plays a guitar, or a recorded song is sometimes used), and we say some simple prayers together. Then each child goes to a quiet learning area for one-on-one work with his or her teen mentor. Teen mentors are trained to establish a routine for work with their students. Homework is given each week. After completing preparation, the students receive the sacraments with the larger religious education group, and often they attend Sunday Mass. Because the children practice the Mass rituals in class, they usually fit in well with the congregation. Occasionally, they join the larger religious education group on field trips.

Sample 45-Minute Schedule	
Typical Steps	Approximate Time
Opening Song or Prayer Whole group: faith mentors, learners, parents, and leaders Mentors and learners go to designated areas for one-on-one work.	5 minutes
Begin with Life Experience The one-on-one lesson starts with the learner's own experience.	10 minutes
Connect Lesson concepts are presented in an approach that is customized for the learner and builds on his or her strengths. Learning tools and hands-on materials are often used.	15 minutes
Close Lesson closes with concept reinforcement and prayer.	10 minutes
Transition for Home Faith mentor talks with parents about "homework" experience for the learner to reinforce the lesson concepts.	5 minutes

The routine doesn't change, but the pace of learning varies for each student. Mentors do not proceed to a new lesson until the student shows a mastery of the current lesson to the best of his or her abilities, which the mentor determines in conjunction with the program coordinator and the child's parents. Progress is steady, if often slow. Some students are not confirmed until they are in their late teens or twenties. But every child with special needs who has stuck with the program has been successfully confirmed; they all receive the Eucharist and the Sacrament of Penance and Reconciliation, and they attend Mass regularly.

Advantages of Individualized Catechesis

The mainstreaming method begins with the regular class and attempts to modify it to suit children with disabilities. In contrast, individualized catechesis succeeds because it is adapted to each child's needs. It doesn't try to fit a child with disabilities into a class of children with similar learning styles and normal sensory-processing abilities. It openly and directly recognizes children's different abilities and needs and accommodates them. Individualized catechesis begins with children with disabilities and designs learning strategies to suit each child's unique abilities and strengths while maintaining a focus on their relationship with God and with others.

Paul's story illustrates the effectiveness of this method. Paul, a seven-year-old with autism, joined the regular religious education program to prepare for First Eucharist. There was trouble from the start. Paul was bright, but he was restless and had a short attention span. The class made him anxious. Periodically, he would get out of his seat, leave the room, and run up and down the hall outside the classroom. Paul's behavior distracted the other children and presented the catechist teaching the class with a difficult dilemma. Should she continue teaching the class or follow Paul and try to get him to return to class?

After a month of this, the director of religious education told Paul's parents that he would not be able to continue in the program. She cited liability concerns—what if Paul left the building?—but it was clear that she thought that there was no way that Paul could successfully stay in the program as it was constructed.

A year later, Paul came into the adaptive religious education program at my parish. We saw that his restlessness was not a behavioral problem but a form of stimming—a response to the rush of sensory data that overwhelmed him in a group setting. The noise, sights, and distractions of the classroom distressed him; he made the problem go away by leaving the room. But once he received instruction in a quiet classroom with a teen mentor who was focused entirely on him, Paul flourished. He received the Eucharist and is progressing toward Confirmation.

Like Paul, most children with autism do not thrive in a regular religious education class in which no modifications are made. Change is difficult for most of these children. They adjust to new environments slowly. Being thrown into a new school with new peers with little structure is difficult. Most children with ASD do not intuitively grasp the rules of a new social situation. They do not understand that others think differently than they do, and they are not adept at the give-and-take that makes for smooth personal relationships. It takes a long time for children with autism to feel comfortable in a classroom full of new people with different personalities. In fact, they may never feel comfortable there.

Take Jimmy, for example. Jimmy has been a good student in our adaptive religious education program for six years, but every new year he has a hard time getting started. Before the first class, he comes in to inspect the classroom and to go over plans for the year with his teen mentor (who has been working with him since his third year). He and the teen mentor spend the first three weeks of class just getting used to each other again. Jimmy does very well once he settles into his routine, but he has never been comfortable with the short group meeting at the beginning of class. I doubt that he would ever be able to participate in a mainstreamed religious education class.

Most children with autism have a strong need for routine and structure (although they do not always feel this need as strongly as Jimmy does). In typical classrooms teachers and catechists set rules, of course, but they usually change the routines to keep children interested. In successive weeks they might show a video, teach a song, play a game, do a small-group craft project, tour the church, and greet the pastor for a special appearance. Interesting, attention-getting innovations like these stimulate most students, but they are disorienting and disconcerting for children with ASD. These children rely on routine and predictability to keep their bearings. Routine anchors them while they attend to surprises such as new children, noise, temperature changes, and the like. Without routines, they suffer in confusion and seem to never become settled.

By necessity, teachers must use some version of the lecture or small-group format to instruct a class of any significant size. This seldom suits the needs of children with autism. The lecture part of the class is aimed at children with typical abilities. The small-group part usually presents a formidable challenge to children with impaired social functioning who may also have auditory and other information-processing problems. They do better with individual attention, but catechists are not always able to work with them individually in the available class time.

The average classroom is a distracting place for children with sensory-processing difficulties. Bright and buzzing lights, loud noises, art projects, colorful streamers and wall hangings, the restless chatter of a room full of children—all of these things overstimulate and distract children who have trouble concentrating. Almost invariably, children with autism will react to this stimulation and confusion by stimming. Stimming disturbs everyone else, thus making the mainstream classroom a difficult learning environment for neurotypical children as well.

Individualized catechesis, though, offers considerable advantages for children with autism and children with some other disabilities.

Benefits of the Individualized Catechesis Method

- establishes trusting relationships
- provides positive near-peer role models
- provides comfort of predictability in human interactions
- is adapted to each student's individual strengths and needs
- fosters acceptance of unplanned behaviors and responses
- offers routine structure
- provides for low-sensory environments based on individual needs
- offers the flexibility to repeat lessons as needed
- fosters inclusive community
- encourages service among parish youth

Relationship Inclusion

Individualized catechesis as we practice it at Our Lady of Grace provides a program of relationships. You might call it a model of relationship inclusion. At the deepest level, it's concerned with building and strengthening the child's relationship with God. This relationship is personal; all children, those with disabilities and those without, can know God's personal love for them. It's also communal; every child relates to God as a member of a community of faith, lived out primarily in his or her local parish. The program nurtures both the personal and the communal dimensions of a relationship with God.

This happens primarily through a special relationship—the relationship between the child and his or her teen faith mentor. Children with autism typically have trouble with personal relationships. Because they have difficulty reading social cues and understanding the effect of their words and actions on others, they are isolated from their peers, who too often respond to kids who are different with indifference or hostility. In individualized catechesis, the main channel of teaching and learning is the intensive, one-on-one relationship between the child and the teen faith mentor. This relationship deepens over time. Often, the faith mentor is the first peer or near peer to take an interest in the child and spend time with him or her. It's common for the children to develop intense relationships of trust and affection with their mentors, which creates the best possible context for the children to learn about a relationship with Jesus.

These bonds develop quite naturally between children and their near-peer faith mentors, like the friendship between Gabe and his mentor, Maria. When he came into the program, Gabe was a very smart ten-year-old with a high-functioning form of autism. He had a short attention span, and he loved to keep people off balance by changing the subject. Maria was just as smart and just as quick. When Gabe changed the subject, she had another lesson ready for him. The two bonded over a video game. Gabe was an expert in a particular game, and he wanted to talk about it all the time. Maria knew the game, too, so she proposed an agreement; whenever Gabe worked on a lesson for ten minutes, Maria would talk to him about the game for three minutes. They clicked. Maria became Gabe's best friend. He made rapid progress in class.

Relationships with teen mentors lead children to a deeper relationship with the parish. Typically, teen mentors lead the practice of our rituals, accompany their students at Mass, and are present when they receive the sacraments. An adaptive religious education program is most effective when accompanied by efforts to make people with disabilities visible in the parish as a whole. It's not unusual for students who have completed the program to become faith mentors themselves. (Yes, people with autism are serving as mentors!) The student-mentor relationship brings healing as well as learning to children with disabilities.

The program positively influences family relationships, too. Parents accompany their children to class and reinforce lessons with them at home. Parents meet for discussion during class time, which forms bonds of support and trust among parents. Quite often, the child's participation in religious education is the occasion for the parents to repair a broken or frayed relationship with the Church. The program emphasizes family prayer and Catholic devotions and imagery in the home. Often, siblings of children in the program become faith mentors in the program.

Finally, let's not overlook the program's positive impact on the faith mentors. The young mentors are drawn into a meaningful role of service in the parish, usually for the first time. They go to Mass regularly. They talk to their students' parents every week. Like all teachers, they learn the material better through the act of teaching it. Many of our faith mentors have moved into other roles of service inside and outside the parish; three have become special education teachers, two are in graduate school studying psychology, one is studying speech pathology, and two more are interested in becoming occupational therapists.

This constellation of new relationships and deepening relationships is an appealing model for the inclusion of children with disabilities in the life of the Church. It is religious education in the finest sense—a path to a deeper relationship with God and other people, accomplished through trust and affection.

> It is religious education in the finest sense—a path to a deeper relationship with God and other people, accomplished through trust and affection.

A Word About Parents

Religious educators often emphasize that effective catechesis is a family affair. The family is the most powerful force in the faith formation of a child. Parents raise their children in the faith. Religious education in the parish is an essential part of this process, but it's not the whole of it. Just as the home supports classroom catechesis, the parish's religious education program can have a powerful influence on the faith life of the family. It's not uncommon for parents to experience a deepening of their own faith as they participate in the religious education of their children.

This is especially true of parents of children with autism and other disabilities. They are different from other parents. When they bring their children to the parish for religious education, they bring a distinctive set of attitudes and needs. Some are scared and defensive. Some blame themselves for their child's disability. Some are ashamed. Some are angry. All of them are grieving. They experienced a profound shock when their child's disability was diagnosed. This may have come at birth (or even before) for children with Down syndrome and other genetic conditions. It comes later for parents of children with autism when problems with learning and behavior become too numerous to ignore. Whenever it comes, parents are shocked and saddened; from that moment on, they face the task of continually adjusting to the changing realities of who their child is. This isn't the child they expected. They must continually accept the fact that their child cannot have what other children have, at least not right away.

Simply being with other parents in a welcoming setting can bring comfort. I think of Carol, the mother of a son with autism. She was sad and withdrawn when she first brought her son to the program. One morning after class she fought back tears as she told me her story. Life at home was difficult. Her husband had stopped going to church. She felt very much alone, especially when she saw three fathers at the parents' table who were involved with their children's religious education. Carol benefited greatly from the program. Her grief eased. She made friends. Today she makes a special point to greet new parents and sit with them.

Parents often mistakenly think that their children don't need or can't have a religious education like other children. Parents who do not have strong religious practices themselves are especially likely to think this way. They might also hold their children back from religious education if they have an overly intellectual view of faith. If they think that being a Catholic mainly means understanding doctrines, they'll likely think that a child with intellectual disabilities and learning problems will be hard pressed to do that.

Parish ministers need to counter these attitudes. Intellectual, physical, or developmental disability doesn't mean spiritual disability. A child who may never grasp the fine points of the Nicene Creed is still capable of understanding who Jesus is. A child who will never memorize the eight Beatitudes or the names of the twelve apostles can enjoy Mass, receive the Eucharist, and learn to be forgiving and generous.

I think of a sunny afternoon at Our Lady of Grace when the young people in our parish were confirmed. One of them was Craig, a thirteen-year-old with a fairly severe form of autism. Craig had been in the individualized catechesis program for five years. I participated in the ceremony as a deacon. When Craig was confirmed, I saw his grandfather standing nearby, tears streaming down his face. Later he told me that he never thought Craig would be confirmed. He thought it was a great gift, a kind of miracle. It was a great gift—to the grandfather as well as to Craig. He had experienced a sacrament as defined by the *Catechism*, an "efficacious sign of grace."

There's no substitute for a welcoming spirit. Our society is full of places that are not especially welcoming to people who are different. The parish should not be one of those places.

4

Roles in the Program

A religious education program using individualized catechesis resembles a football team or an acting troupe. For the program to succeed, many people playing different roles have to work together smoothly. The spotlight is on the relationship between faith mentors and their students. They are the players on the field or the actors on the stage; their work is what everyone comes to see. The program coordinator orchestrates and supports the action, like the coach on the sidelines or the director of the play. The pastor of the parish and the director of religious education are the producers; they make the show possible. Parents, family members, and other people in the parish are the audience, watching intently; it's an audience that has an active role to play in the program, too.

In this chapter, I discuss these roles. I want to emphasize that success comes only when everyone works together. If we get too focused on roles, job descriptions, and responsibilities, we lose sight of the larger picture. The point of this is to bring children to the fullest degree of spiritual maturity of which they are capable. A closely related goal is to help the parents and families of these children live an active life of faith. The larger picture is easy to see; one of the attractions of the program is the satisfaction of seeing progress every week.

A Pastoral Attitude

The most desirable quality for everyone involved in the program is a pastoral attitude. Pastors take the broad view. They act for the long-term good rather than short-term efficiency. They are decisive when they need to be, patient with difficulty, and compassionate in the face of suffering. All of us can strive to approach our work with a pastoral mind-set. The root meaning of *pastor* is "shepherd." Jesus described himself as the "good shepherd" who would lay down his life for the good of the flock but who was also willing to go to any length to save an individual who wandered away. That's the skill of a pastor: moving the group toward a common goal while caring for each person individually.

A pastoral attitude is the remedy for the considerable anxiety that participants bring to the program. Social unease and general uncertainty is common among children with autism. Many are in a perpetual state of anxiety. They can't predict what other people are going to do, and they lack the ability to quickly understand new social situations. They struggle to figure out what is expected of them. School is especially fraught with uncertainty.

It's no surprise that parents are typically apprehensive and tense as they bring their children to religious education. Their children may have been ignored, teased, and even bullied by other students in school. Parents might have seen how teachers and other adults are uneasy with their kids. Many aren't sure that religious education will work for their children at all. They wonder, "Will the mentor 'get' my child?" The teen mentors are also anxious. Teenagers like to test new things gradually from a base of security and familiarity. Teen faith mentors in the program are thrown into a situation where everything is new. They're often assuming their first role of service. They're building a relationship with a child who reacts in unfamiliar ways. They're being called on to relate to adults in an adult manner. It's a challenging, often fragile situation. Those in charge of it need a pastor's heart.

One family I know suffered a double pastoral failure. Their son Paul, the seven-year-old with autism I mentioned previously, had a hard time in a regular religious education class. He was in the habit of getting out of his seat and wandering around the classroom. Several times he left the room. The alarmed program director expelled the boy from the program, citing concerns about the parish's liability if the boy wandered out into the street. The boy's father, angered by the decision, stopped coming to church for some months. One Sunday he returned to Mass. Then one of the parish ministers greeted him and said he knew that the man hadn't been to church lately; he said, "I noticed that your envelopes haven't been in the collection for a while." The remark infuriated the father, who once again stopped coming to Mass.

Another parish minister reached out to the hurt and angry father. Eventually, he enrolled his son in the individualized catechesis program. I found that the fears about the boy's safety were exaggerated; he would never have left the building, much less wandered into the street. He did, however, need to learn to stay in the classroom. He gradually learned this lesson through the patient work of a teen faith mentor who built a trusting and close relationship with him. The boy's father had a lot to get off his chest. Over the course of time, he was heard during the weekly parents' meeting. He was able to return to Mass and has become active in the parish again.

The Pastor's Role

The pastor is the chief shepherd of the parish, and his support is essential to any adaptive religious education program. His involvement can take several forms. Some pastors take the lead. Services for people with disabilities are a priority for them. Pastors might initiate the individualized catechesis program, encourage their staff to implement it, and take a hands-on role. More often, someone else initiates the program—the catechetical leader, a deacon, or other parish staff. Typically, this person acts in response to parishioners who have asked that their children with disabilities be prepared for the sacraments. Someone on the parish staff takes up the issue, discovers that a significant number of children could benefit, and decides to talk about starting a program.

The question quickly comes to the pastor, whose support is essential if the idea is to go forward. The pastor needs to understand that any religious education program for children with disabilities might cause disruptions and ruffle some feathers. It means that children with autism and other disabilities will be present at Mass. Their fidgeting and vocal stimming can be reduced but not eliminated, and some people accustomed to their "quiet Mass" will complain. There are likely to be questions about whether the parish should invest so much effort in a program that benefits relatively few people. Some will ask why "God's special children" need religious education at all. There will be doubts about relying on teenagers to instruct; questions about the need for special expertise in autism and other intellectual, physical, or developmental disabilities; concerns about safety and order in class. At every point, the pastor needs to stand solidly behind the choice of welcoming all parishioners with disabilities into the full life of the parish. This can include starting an adaptive religious education program using an individualized catechesis method. The pastor needs to be a friend to persons with disabilities.

Then there is the upheaval and change that any new program brings. In my parish, the adaptive religious education program made a sizable footprint on Sunday mornings. We needed a lot of space for one-on-one instruction, so we took over rooms that other classes and parish activities had used. Our pastor heard many complaints. Through it all, he never wavered in his support for the program.

Much of the pastor's role consists of this kind of behind-the-scenes support and advocacy. He needs to be informed about the program in order to defend and support it. He does not need to be an expert in disabilities, and he does not need to take a highly visible hands-on role. Pastors have plenty to do. With good people in charge, an adaptive religious education program does not have to be a drain on the pastor's time.

The pastor does get directly involved in the program when administering the sacraments. The most challenging is the Sacrament of Penance and Reconciliation. The sacrament goes differently for children with limited language, impaired social skills, and sometimes intellectual deficits. The priest must be willing to learn how to communicate with these children and understand what they say. In our program, the teen mentors or program coordinator help the priest learn how to effectively and efficiently communicate so that the sacrament can be successfully administered.

The pastor may have to say a special Mass for children with especially severe disabilities. Our pastor did this for several children in our program who are too sensitive to visual and auditory stimulation to attend a regular Mass comfortably.

The Catechetical Leader's Role

It is the responsibility of a parish's catechetical leader or director of religious education to ensure that any child with a disability receives an appropriate religious education. An adaptive religious education program should be considered an integral part of the total parish program. The catechetical leader should work closely with the program coordinator and should review and approve the curriculum. The catechetical leader must, in consultation with the program coordinator and mentor, ensure a child's readiness for the sacraments. The catechetical leader ensures that all teen faith mentors and volunteers fulfill any necessary safe-environment requirements. When appropriate, the catechetical leader sees that the teen mentors receive the same orientation and training as parish volunteer catechists, in addition to any specialized training that is needed, including catechetical certification. In addition, the catechetical leader collaborates with the program coordinator to review the annual schedule and to integrate the children into parish events.

The Program Coordinator's Role

The program coordinator plays a key role. He or she is the go-to person. You might compare the program coordinator to the director and stage manager of a play—the person responsible for determining sets, casting, lighting, script, schedule, and everything else. Ordinarily, the director of religious education should not try to be the adaptive program coordinator as well. As the tasks and problems are different from those of typical religious education classes, I believe the best arrangement is for the catechetical leader to be in overall charge of all religious education, including the adaptive religious education program, but to leave the administration of the program up to the coordinator.

The program coordinator might be a professional in the field of developmental disabilities and perhaps (but not necessarily) a member of the parish. Such a person has to be a Catholic in good standing and will likely work with the catechetical leader, school principal, or pastor as co-coordinators. Sometimes a parent or other relative of a child with disabilities will apply for the job of program coordinator. The parent might be the spark who got the parish staff interested in starting a program, and he or she may be a highly articulate, knowledgeable, and vocal advocate for the interests of children with disabilities. Although firsthand experience of the strains and challenges of raising a child with a disability may be helpful, it's not a core requirement. Other qualifications are more important.

Religious Education Experience

Chief among the important qualifications for a program coordinator to have is religious education experience. The coordinator needs to have a strong background in the religious education of young people, including preparation for the Sacraments of the Eucharist, Reconciliation, and Confirmation and the major topics covered in the curriculum. The coordinator needs to understand the curriculum and what the adaptations to it are trying to accomplish. Communicating spiritual concepts to children with a range of disabilities calls for considerable creativity and ingenuity, and adaptations will be successful only if they are firmly grounded in an understanding of the principles and methods of Catholic religious education. The program coordinator must understand those principles thoroughly and be able to communicate that understanding to teen faith mentors. Any curriculum adaptation should, like the *Adaptive Finding God Program*, include consistent instruction; it should provide customized strategies to build on a variety of strengths, and communication and learning styles; and it should include learning tools to make catechetical concepts concrete.

Working with Teens

The coordinator must be good at recruiting and training teen faith mentors. Most teens have misgivings about the idea of becoming a mentor in an individualized catechesis program. The most common objection is, "I don't know enough about religion to teach anybody about it." Most teens are apprehensive about the prospect of working closely with a disabled child. Further, teens tend to be shy about relating to adults, and individualized catechesis requires them to work closely with the student's parents.

These doubts are not without foundation, and successful program coordinators can overcome them with inspiration, encouragement, reassurance, and warmth. Successful coordinators are able to assure teens that they know more about their faith than they think and that they possess the talents to build relationships with their students and their students' parents. They need to make sure that teens know that they will get the training they need to be effective mentors. Encouragement is most crucial at the beginning. Once the teen faith mentors begin to work, their student will likely keep them motivated and focused.

It's especially important for the program coordinator to match students with the right mentor. Take your time with this. Don't be afraid to try different combinations of mentors and students. Look for natural synergy. Often the mentor will find a solution to a problem that has eluded everyone else.

This was the case with Derek, a bright boy with autism who was extremely distractible. He would pay attention to a mentor for a minute or so before his attention would begin to wander. We tried various tactics, but nothing seemed to help until a teen mentor named Jake came in one day with a small whiteboard and a marker. Derek paid close attention as soon as Jake showed him the board. Jake wrote a question; Derek wrote an answer. The board was a focusing device; it was the solution we'd been looking for. Jake became Derek's teen faith mentor, and they worked their way through the lessons by writing on the whiteboard.

Knowledge of Special Needs

The program coordinator needs to know about autism and how it affects learning and social interaction. This doesn't have to be the knowledge of a professional in special education with firsthand experience. But the coordinator must know enough about autism to be able to guide a curriculum adapted for these children and to create a learning environment suited for them.

I am convinced that any capable religious educator who is well organized, able to work with teenagers, and possesses a heart for this work can acquire the necessary knowledge of disabilities with a reasonable investment of time. In my travels helping dioceses and parishes implement the individualized catechesis method, people often note that few parishes will have a program coordinator with the expertise that I have. I'm an ordained deacon with a doctorate and a license to practice psychology, and I have extensive professional experience working with people with autism. One diocesan official told me that an adaptive religious education program "is easy for a parish with someone like you. How can an ordinary parish do it?" I responded that it's not easy even in my parish, but I also told him that virtually every parish can acquire the expertise it needs in a reasonable period of time with focused effort.

The necessary training often comes from local people. Many communities of any size in the Unites States have at least some services for people with disabilities. In many communities, these services are quite extensive. They are provided by social workers, psychologists, special education teachers, occupational therapists, speech and language pathologists, and other professionals, most of whom are eager to assist anyone who wants to help people with disabilities learn and flourish. In fact, working with families, educators, employers, clergy, and other community leaders is part of the job description of most of these professionals. They are available for workshops, orientation sessions, and consultation. Parents of children with disabilities are often quite knowledgeable and willing to share their expertise with the coordinator and other parish staff. Parishes can also often draw on diocesan staff in charge of disability services and coordinators of nearby religious education programs that serve children with developmental disabilities. In addition, the website for the National Catholic Partnership on Disability has invaluable resources for catechesis.

Administrative-Managerial Ability

The coordinator oversees a highly decentralized program in which change is happening constantly: instruction is individualized; every student and every mentor is different; every parent seems to have a question every week; adjustments large and small are being made constantly. Coordinators of an adaptive religious education program must be able to handle a constant flow of questions, decisions, and problems. At times they'll feel like they're experts in navigating chaos.

Facilities The coordinator needs to make sure that the rooms used for this program are suitable for this type of learning. Ideally, rooms should be quiet, with subdued lighting, and allow for only a minimum of distraction. Practically, this often means that the coordinator needs to get there early to arrange classrooms for the program and stay late to make sure they are returned to their original condition afterward. If you do not have multiple classrooms available, you can divide a room using desks or dividers.

Planning The coordinator must be well organized and able to plan ahead. He or she must set the calendar for the program well in advance. The calendar needs to include sessions for orientation of teens, parents, and students; training of teen mentors; and meetings with parents. The program must be coordinated with the parish calendar and with the schedule for the standard religious education class for events done together, like Mass and the sacraments. The coordinator will frequently juggle schedules to accommodate busy students and mentors.

Availability The coordinator must be available to parents, teen mentors, and parish staff. I give my e-mail and telephone number to mentors and parents, and I insist that they let me and one another know when a student or mentor will miss a class because of sickness or other unavoidable obligation. The program coordinator must also be able to reach everybody quickly when there is a last-minute change in class for weather-related reasons.

Keeper of Materials The program will generate a considerable amount of material—lessons, visual aids, resource books, magazines, and handouts. The program coordinator needs to prepare this material and distribute it, often in advance. And don't forget the paper, pencils, crayons, and other supplies that any school program needs!

Parents The coordinator oversees the plan for the parents who accompany their children. In my program parents sit together for a facilitated discussion with a counselor while their children are working with their faith mentors.

The Near-Peer Faith Mentor's Role

Again, the key to the program's success is the relationship that develops between the student and the teen mentor. When that relationship is close and meaningful, students learn. When it falters, students make fitful progress or none at all. It's no exaggeration to say that the most important helper in the program is the teen faith mentor.

The idea of using teenagers as faith mentors was something of an experiment when I started the program. I had seen religious education programs that used one-on-one instruction, and I was familiar with programs that involved adolescents as teaching assistants and aides. But I had never seen a program that combined the two, using teens for individualized instruction. In my professional work, I had observed that children with autism seemed to learn best from people their own age or close to it. A bond seemed to form that facilitated learning. I thought that teens might relate more easily to children with autism because they lack the prejudices and expectations—and also the self-doubt—that many adults seem to have. If so, they might be able to develop a personal relationship with these students that would make learning easier.

These suppositions proved correct. But I didn't anticipate what has turned out to be the most important outcome of using teens as mentors—the way mentors become role models for their students. Most children in the adaptive religious education program form strong bonds with their mentors. They come into the program looking for help. And sadly, many don't have many similar-aged friends; they don't really know how to "make friends" with someone. They are unsure of themselves, anxious, and lost in social situations they don't understand. Along comes the faith mentor, a cheerful young person close in age, interested in the student, and happy to spend time with them every week. Students quickly become attached to their mentors. They work hard to please the mentors. They watch how their mentor dresses, talks, and relates to adults and other mentors. The faith mentor becomes a model for how to be in the world.

I saw a powerful example of this outside of class. Twice a year, the Pittsburgh Penguins hockey team gives our program the use of a luxury box at their arena, Consol Energy Center. Everybody—students, mentors, and some adult chaperones—goes to the hockey game for a night of fun. One season, I noticed that Billy, one of our older students, didn't seem to be enjoying himself very much. He sat a little apart; he watched the others fooling around and cheering when the Penguins scored a goal, but he didn't join in himself. A few months later we went back for another game. This time Billy joined right in with everyone else. I realized that during the first game, Billy had been learning how to have fun. He had carefully observed what people do at hockey games. The second time he put what he observed into effect. It may have been deliberate imitation, but Billy seemed to be having a great time.

This is for real. The mentors' first responsibility is to understand how important they are to their students. Frequently, teens don't realize how quickly their students come to depend on them. It's a relationship they need to take seriously. They need to know that their students are watching them carefully and will imitate what they see. Being a role model and mentor for children with autism requires a great deal of responsibility.

Know the student. The mentor gets to know his or her student very well, often better than anyone outside the student's family. They learn what "stims" really mean. They learn how the child communicates. They get to know how the child learns best. This is subtle knowledge. Children with autism don't communicate the way most people do. They often can't tell you that they would rather look at pictures than listen to you read from a book, that they don't like to be touched, or that loud noises disturb them. The mentor learns such things gradually, through patient observation and trial and error. Over time the mentor gleans how the child learns and is able to develop an effective approach to teaching.

Manage time well. The mentor needs to be on time, arrive at class prepared to teach, and teach with a good understanding of the purpose of the lesson. He or she needs to be in good communication with the coordinator and the student's parents. The mentor needs to review and prepare the lesson with the program coordinator before he or she arrives at the weekly meeting.

Work with parents. Parents know their children better than anyone else does. Teen faith mentors work closely with parents when they are first getting to know their students, and the relationship continues throughout the program. Mentors review the weekly lessons with parents so parents can repeat the lessons at home during the week. Parents and teen faith mentors need to communicate about schedules. Sometimes mentors need to talk to parents about difficulties their children are having. This relationship is something of a role reversal. Some teens take to it naturally. Most need coaching and respond well to it. Often the program coordinator will need to help facilitate this relationship between teen mentors and parents.

Parents' Role

Parents are required to participate in the program with their children. There are practical reasons for this. Parents help mentors understand how their children learn and communicate. Often, the children need to have their parents nearby for stability and reassurance, especially in the early weeks of the program, which often are difficult. Teen faith mentors meet with parents at the end of each class, and parents are asked to repeat the lesson at home at least once during the week. At Our Lady of Grace, we encourage an active faith life at home. We ask families to observe the seasons of Advent and Lent, we supply materials for family prayers and devotions, and we ask parents to attend Mass with their children. The hope is that the child's participation in the adaptive program will be an occasion for the entire family to deepen their faith life.

In my experience, this happens if parents stick with the program. It usually takes time. The parents of our students cope with strains and disappointments that are far greater than the usual pressures on families. Over time, as their children receive the sacraments and grow in faith, most parents deepen their own faith as well. Facilitating this healing is deeply gratifying.

I recall Dominic, a father who did everything the program asked of him but with an edge. He brought his son to class but didn't interact with other parents easily. He didn't go to Mass. Over time, as his son learned about his faith, Dominic loosened up. He told me one day that I had been "on trial" for two years. He had been hurt by and angry with the Church because of the thoughtless way some pastoral ministers had treated his son. He had brought his son to the program because his wife insisted that he do it. He didn't think the program would work. He had been watching me and the teen mentor carefully, waiting for the disappointment he'd come to expect. Instead, he found a program that helped his son and in the process gave him a way back into the Catholic community. I remember the big smile on Dominic's face when he and his son received Holy Communion together.

Dominic's story illustrates another important aspect of the program: success takes time. A spirit of patient trust is an essential virtue. It takes time to develop a program. It takes time for mentors to find the best way to teach. Children make progress at their own pace. This program is an opportunity for everyone involved—coordinators, pastors, mentors, parents, and students—to practice the virtue of patience in a culture that demands immediate results.

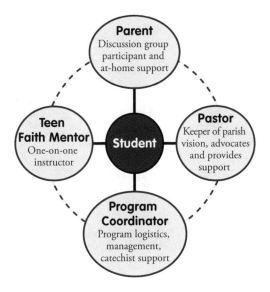

5

Starting a Program

The key decision makers in your parish have made the decision: you want to implement an adaptive religious education program for children with autism and other special needs. How do you get started? What's involved? How long will it take? What are the things to watch out for? To continue the theatrical analogy, this chapter is about the work involved in getting a show ready for opening night. The actors are merely the players on stage. People who are literally behind the scenes—writers, electricians, stagehands, dressmakers, producers and directors and their staffs—do much of the work.

This chapter is about getting the show ready for opening night. The next chapter is about keeping the show going.

The Scope

Most people reading this book know about parish programs. You know how complex they can be; how challenging it is to find, train, and motivate volunteers; and what it feels like to have a seemingly endless list of details needing immediate attention. Nevertheless, I want to emphasize the broad scope of our program. Offering individualized instruction to children with autism and other disabilities is a logical extension of an existing religious education program. But while it is integral to a parish's religious education offerings, it comes with its own unique characteristics and challenges. It serves parish families coping with challenges that most families never face.

This broadens the scope of the challenges facing catechetical leaders. Every child's impairment is different, as are his or her strengths and abilities. Each child reacts differently and learns differently. Every child must be taught in a way that suits his or her unique abilities and learning style. In typical religious education classes, a catechist makes choices that help the whole class. With individualized catechesis, each decision about instruction is based on the needs of a single child.

Preparing the Parish

Starting a program that uses individualized catechesis is easier when the parish is alert to the needs of people with disabilities and is accustomed to seeing them in visible, active roles in the parish. It's easier to recruit teen faith mentors, easier for parents to come forward with their children, and easier to get funding and pastoral support. It's easier to achieve the ultimate goal of this program, which is to bring young people with autism and other disabilities into the fullest degree of spiritual maturity of which they are capable and to see them integrated into the local parish community.

Crucial in the preparation for an adaptive religious education program is parish awareness and the steady advocacy for the needs of parishioners with disabilities. The goal is a parish community that eagerly seeks out, embraces, and welcomes people with disabilities, young and old alike. People with disabilities—especially children—aren't much in evidence in our parishes. They often don't rank high in the list of groups and causes that parishioners are typically exhorted to support: young people, older people, singles, young professionals, single mothers, people who are homeless or those who are grieving, disaster relief, pro-life, evangelization, among others. Paying sufficient attention to people with disabilities requires intentional effort.

The pastor and other clergy need to take the lead in this, and they need to do it in the right way. Often parish leaders will seek support for parishioners with disabilities (and other special groups) by insisting, "Our parish must be open to everyone." This is certainly true; including people with disabilities in parish life (and in society as a whole) is a requirement of justice. But the assertion that a parish must be open to everyone is a very general statement that is heard quite often in connection with many groups with particular identities and special needs. This attitude needs to be supported with practical action.

Effective advocacy for people with disabilities can often be quite subtle, rendered with little fanfare. Parish leaders can simply mention people with disabilities in a natural, unforced way whenever they can. They can draw attention to their needs by providing large-print Mass materials, providing interpreters at Mass, ensuring that parish events are accessible to people in wheelchairs, and supporting local organizations that serve people with disabilities. They can take small steps to make people with disabilities visible, comfortable, and involved. As I mentioned, in my parish a man with autism has been an usher at the 9:30 a.m. Mass for fifteen years. A man with a hearing impairment is a lector. When pastors speak about people with disabilities from the pulpit they can remind their parishioners that virtually everyone will cope with a disability at some point in his or her life.

In a welcoming parish, individualized catechesis is a natural outgrowth of a long-standing concern for the needs of people with disabilities. The reverse is also true; the adaptive religious education program can promote the well-being of parishioners with disabilities in other ways. At the Our Lady of Grace parish, the adaptive religious education program on Sunday mornings gradually led to the 9:30 Mass becoming a time where people with disabilities feel at home. At this Mass, their presence in the parish is especially visible. It's a noisy Mass. A child periodically runs in the aisles. Others flap their hands. At every

Mass someone is sure to make noise when quiet is called for. But it's OK. These children and adults are not only at home in their parish; they make it whole.

Does Your Parish Need a Program?

Parish ministers need to determine the need for an adaptive religious education program. If a child presents him- or herself to a parish, we need to address the child's needs. The average parish almost certainly has children with special needs. These parishioners include children at the usual ages for sacramental preparation, teens and adults who have never been confirmed, and even some who have never received the Eucharist and Reconciliation.

Potential students may be there, but identifying them is another matter. They may reside within parish boundaries but not attend Mass. As noted earlier, parents are reluctant to bring forward their disabled children for religious education. They are protective of their children. Their kids don't fit in. They've been teased and bullied at school and in other social settings. They are sensitive about the label "disabled." It carries a stigma and can make it difficult for the child to fit in.

Many parents simply assume that their children aren't eligible for religious education. Their children usually receive special education services in the public schools, and they've dealt with therapists, special education teachers, classroom aides, and other specialists. Since these supports aren't available in parish religious education programs, parents might assume that their children won't be able to learn in this setting. It's also the case that parents can underestimate their child's abilities. In my professional work, I have often seen children perform much better than people expected them to. With a focused, individualized, child-centered method, remarkable things can occur. Children need time and patient encouragement—and the opportunity to express themselves.

Many parents don't think about religious education until their child reaches the age to receive First Eucharist. (This is true for parents of all children.) Some parents might approach a parish minister to talk about it. Many will not. It's a bold move for anyone to approach the pastor and ask the parish to provide a special service. Parents need to be invited.

Parish ministers can make good use of private networks and personal contacts to find these parents. Members of the parish staff may know some of them already and can recommend they ask for religious education. There are likely members of the parish who work with people with autism professionally as teachers, speech or occupational therapists, psychologists, or social workers. Many children in the program in my parish came because I got to know them in my work as a psychologist specializing in autism spectrum disorders. I'm not unique. Identify and consult with parishioners who work with people with autism and other disabilities.

The program at Our Lady of Grace began with five students. Your program, like mine, will probably grow over time as word gets out. Over a few years, my parish's program gradually grew to about fifteen students. Then the numbers suddenly shot up to twenty and then twenty-five.

You might consider the possibility of operating the adaptive religious education program jointly with another parish (or several parishes). This adds a layer of complexity to planning, but it enlarges the pool of potential students and brings more human and material resources into the picture. Many diocesan bishops strongly encourage joint programs and the pooling of resources among parishes. Offering religious education to young people with disabilities is an obvious way that parishes can work together.

Word will spread. If you offer an adaptive religious education program on your own, expect parents from other parishes to come knocking on your door. You might want to decide in advance how you will handle this. Our Lady of Grace accepts everyone into the program regardless of parish membership. Some families travel long distances on Sunday mornings to be part of it. Of course, this is not the ideal. Every parish has a responsibility to serve the needs of its parishioners. And we're ready to help any parish that wishes to start an adaptive religious education program of its own. A dozen dioceses in the eastern United States have begun formal review of a program using the individualized catechesis method, and several parishes are formally offering it as a parish religious education program. The development of the *Adaptive Finding God Program* makes it possible for every parish to respond meaningfully to each family in need.

Publicize the Program

When it's time to announce the adaptive religious education program, do it strongly, not quietly. The pastor or catechetical leader should speak about it from the pulpit at all the Sunday Masses. It should be presented as an important new initiative that is part of the parish's broad commitment to meeting the needs of people with disabilities.

It's important to quickly follow up this announcement with an information session where parents can learn more.

How to publicize and recruit.

- Speak from the pulpit about the program.
- Seek out parishioners who are professionals in special needs education and therapy or government agencies.
- Schedule an informational meeting.
- Use all communications channels, including the parish's website, social media, e-mail lists, and bulletin.
- Visit local schools; talk to counselors.

This information session is crucial. There's a lot to explain, and parents need the opportunity to talk. Every child with a developmental disability is unique. Each needs an instructional approach suited to his or her personal style of learning and method of communicating. You might be surprised by the turnout for these sessions. I have participated in many of them; often parents wait patiently for a long time to have the opportunity for a private discussion with the program coordinator.

Use all the communication channels at your disposal. Place announcements in the bulletin. Put a description of the program on your parish website. Invite parish members who work in special education to let their Catholic clients know about the program. Announce the program in other parishes. Several families in our program first heard about it through an article I wrote in our diocesan newspaper.

Schedule

At Our Lady of Grace, the adaptive religious education program is held on Sunday mornings. I think this is the best time for a program that uses teens as faith mentors. There are too many competing activities for teens on Sunday afternoons.

When I decided to schedule the program from 8:30 to 9:15 a.m., several people warned me, "You'll never get teenagers to get up so early on a Sunday morning." These fears have proved exaggerated. Mentors do occasionally come to class shaking off sleep, but they've been quite capable of rising to the challenge of showing up at 8:30 ready to teach, particularly after they've met and made a connection with their student.

I chose the time because it makes it easy for families and mentors to attend the 9:30 Mass. Many children with disabilities (and their parents and siblings) do not attend Mass regularly. Mass is a sore point for many parents of children with autism and other disabilities. Many of their children have trouble sitting still. Sometimes they stim because they are overstimulated, anxious, or bored. Parents don't like annoyed looks (or worse, negative comments) from parishioners who are used to a "quiet" Mass. You can understand why many choose to stay home. As I mentioned, the 9:30 Mass gradually became "our" Mass, and it's now a comfortable place for parents and children to worship.

I also wanted to make it easy for the mentors to attend Mass. Teenagers can fall out of the habit of attending Sunday Mass, and I wanted the program to lead to attendance at Mass. Many of our mentors attend 9:30 Mass with their students since it immediately follows class.

Forty-five minutes of class time doesn't sound like much, but it's sufficient for what we need to do. One-on-one instruction is intense. So that's enough time for the mentors, and it's enough time for the students, some of whom have limited attention spans.

Class begins promptly at 8:30. We sing a song together, accompanied by a parent who plays the guitar. We pray a couple of short prayers. Then mentors and students go off for their sessions. At the end, mentors meet briefly with parents to explain the lesson, so that parents can reinforce it with their children at home during the week.

It's a good idea to make firm decisions about scheduling at the beginning; don't think that you will "see how it goes" and change the schedule later. Change is very upsetting for many children with autism. They rely on routine and can become alarmed when a routine changes. One year I decided to open class with the Lord's Prayer instead of the Hail Mary, as we had done the previous year. This disturbed one boy, who insisted that I was saying the "wrong prayer." I hastily reinstated the Hail Mary, but the boy still watches me carefully every week to make sure I say it.

Facilities

Most children with autism do not thrive in an ordinary, crowded classroom. Because their sensory-processing abilities are often impaired, sights, sounds, and smells, as well as new things in the new classroom and school, overwhelm and confuse them. They have trouble separating important information from background noise. Many are hypersensitive to certain stimuli. Some fixate on seemingly irrelevant details. They are prone to distraction. Mentors work hard to keep their students focused on the lesson, and the learning environment shouldn't make this task any more difficult than it already is.

I use the classrooms of our parish school for the program. No more than two pairs of students and mentors are in a room at one time. Because many young people with autism are hypersensitive to stimuli, we work hard to eliminate sights, sounds, and smells that most people barely perceive. We use natural light as much as possible, because many students are bothered by the faint buzz of fluorescent light fixtures. This makes for dim classrooms on gray Sundays during the winter in Pittsburgh. In warm weather we don't use fans for cooling because the spinning blades of electric fans distract many children with autism. Flowers are another distraction because many children are exceptionally sensitive to scents. We remove as many colorful banners, wall hangings, toys, and play equipment as is practical.

The preschool and nursery classrooms in our school are full of beautiful equipment. One has an elaborate castle that takes up one-third of the room. We've never been able to use these rooms in our program because the furnishings are so distracting.

In the first few years of the program, I used the parish school library. This was a large, quiet, carpeted space that worked well for a small program. However, it didn't work so well for a bright boy named Liam who had high-functioning autism. Liam loved books, he collected books, and they constantly distracted him from his lesson. Liam's mentor solved the problem by making a deal: he could look at books for five minutes if he first worked on his lesson for ten minutes. It worked like a charm. Liam held up his end of the bargain and made sure the mentor stuck to hers.

Even when rooms are prepared well, children with autism are still prone to distractions. I try to help mentors work with these distractions rather than fight against them. An example is Marcus, a boy who became fascinated with the view out the large window in his classroom. In the first few weeks of class, he would constantly leave his seat, walk to the window, and stand there, staring at the cars and people outside. The clever mentor soon stopped trying to get Marcus to come back to his seat; instead, she joined him at the window and taught him there and that's where they are every week, talking about Jesus and the sacraments while looking at the world outside.

The boy at the window is a good example of one principle of effective teaching of children with autism: let the student set some of the rules. In a regular classroom, neurotypical children are expected to conform themselves to the teacher's rules. In our adaptive religious education program, mentors adjust to the students. If a student needs to get up and walk around every five minutes, then teaching takes place in five-minute bursts. If a student has to look out the window, that's where the mentor goes, too.

Getting Off the Ground

The first three classes are crucial. Mentors and students need at least this much time to get to know one another. Mentors must understand their student's unique personality and learning style, and students must do something that few of them have ever done before—establish a relationship with a friend. This relationship is the key to the success of the program; the foundation for it is laid during the first weeks.

The first month of the program can be difficult. Children with autism typically dislike new situations. Adjustment is hard for both new students and for those who have been in the program for a while. It takes time, and there's no way to speed it up appreciably. It is likely that during the first two or three weeks, not much content will be covered, since the mentor and student will be relationship building. It takes as long as it takes. The program coordinator can help by setting a routine for class that doesn't vary from week to week.

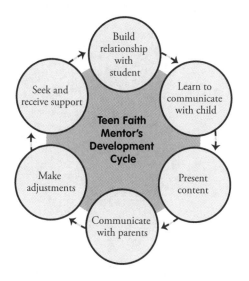

The program coordinator should work intensively with the mentors during this time to help them learn how their students communicate and learn. It's very important that mentors and students be matched well. Sometimes it's necessary to make a switch. Occasionally, I bring in a second mentor to help with a particular student. I pay special attention to helping mentors budget their time well. They need to come to class prepared to teach; they need to allow time to meet with parents after class and get to the 9:30 Mass on time.

It looks like a difficult balancing act. The people in charge of the program must, on the one hand, establish clear expectations and predictable routines. On the other hand, they need to set up a radically decentralized and individualized program tailored to each student's needs. But this is not an impossible task. You can do it, too.

6

Working with Parents, Students, and Teen Faith Mentors

Imagine that you are the program coordinator for a parish that uses individualized catechesis. You've launched the program; now you must run and develop it. Prepare for growth. Chances are the program will be successful. Your success will be noted as young people with developmental disabilities receive the Eucharist and Reconciliation and are confirmed. Parents will be pleased; some might even be astonished at what their children have accomplished. Word will spread, and more parents will come knocking on your door. With more students comes the need for more mentors, more space, more materials, and more meetings. You will be running a program with many moving parts and many constituencies.

There are challenges and issues you will face as the program goes forward. The most important are developing the program content, working with parents, recruiting and training teen faith mentors, and helping them work effectively with students. These are the known challenges. You will never be prepared for everything. There will always be surprises.

I was surprised on the first warm spring Sunday during the program's first year. I turned on the overhead fan in the library before class started. A boy named Timmy came in and became hypnotized by the spinning blades, so I turned the fan off. Timmy left the room, went into another classroom, and turned on the fan. I followed him and turned it off. Timmy went to the next classroom, and the next, and the next, turning the fans on; I followed and turned them all off. Timmy returned to class only after he had turned on the fans in all fifteen classrooms in the building. I was taken by surprise, even though I knew from my professional work that people with autism are often fascinated by spinning things. Now we know. I call it the Timmy rule: never turn on fans in the rooms being used for the adaptive religious education program.

Practicing Rituals

It's important to adapt to children's needs—hence the term *adaptive*. One such adaptation is the practicing of sacramental rituals before the students receive the sacrament. In our first year of the program, four of the five students were preparing to receive the Eucharist. As First Eucharist drew near, I decided to have the students practice receiving Holy Communion. This practice has turned out to be one of the most important features of sacramental preparation.

Practicing the ritual is important because children with autism become anxious in new situations. Receiving Holy Communion for the first time can be an exceptionally anxious experience; practice reduces the number of unknowns and helps children become accustomed to this new thing. Observing and practicing also demonstrates reverent behavior to children who are often concrete thinkers who have difficulty with abstract concepts such as reverence. I begin by having the teen mentors walk through the correct way to receive Holy Communion: process with hands together in prayer, bow before approaching the Eucharistic minister, extend their hands for the host, and say "Amen" in response to "The Body of Christ." The students watch all this intently; then they line up and do the same. Most are visual learners. They "get it" when they see it.

Our class practices receiving the Holy Communion in January and again in March as First Eucharist time approaches. We practice together as a group, older children who have already received their First Eucharist along with the younger ones. Teen faith mentors serve as practice Eucharistic ministers. (One of my hidden agendas is getting teen mentors to think about taking on other roles of service in the parish, such as becoming extraordinary ministers of Holy Communion.)

The Eucharist is the only sacrament we practice together. Students preparing for Confirmation practice the sacrament individually, with mentors playing the roles of bishop and sponsor.

Practicing the Sacrament of Penance and Reconciliation is somewhat more involved. Many children are not able to memorize the prayers that are usually part of the sacrament, and many of them have difficulty grasping the concept of sin. Sin involves the breach of a relationship, and children with autism have trouble understanding the needs, motives, and feelings of others. Mentors often draw parents into the process of preparation. They can provide examples of behavior with family members at home that help the child understand what to bring to God for forgiveness.

Although challenging, we have successfully prepared children with little or no verbal language for the Sacrament of Penance and Reconciliation. My teen mentors have become very good at teaching our pastor how to communicate with their students, so that confession takes place.

The Liturgical Year

Like all religious education programs, the adaptive program pays attention to the liturgical seasons of Advent, Christmas, Lent, and Holy Week and Easter. The seasons are very popular with the students.

They like the Advent wreath, candles, Christmas tree, ashes, crucifix, and other objects and symbols connected with the liturgical seasons.

In our program, we suspend regular lessons in early December for two sessions on Advent and one on the birth of Jesus. I display a giant Advent wreath and demonstrate lighting and extinguishing the candles. The candles are an immediate hit with the students. Everyone has to take a turn blowing out the candles. I also do two sessions on Lent and one on the Resurrection.

I introduce these lessons myself (with the help of mentors) at the beginning of class in which parents as well as students are present. I find it very important that basic concepts are conveyed and that parents hear them and follow or practice them during these special seasons. The sessions on the liturgical year are good opportunities to encourage parents to introduce Catholic prayer and devotions into their family life.

Supplemental Materials

When I started the program, I did not anticipate how important supplies and supplemental materials would become. Most of our students are visual learners. Some learn this way exclusively. When using an individualized catechesis method, it's often beneficial for mentors to use hands-on learning tools that engage but do not distract or cause anxiety for the student. For years, faith mentors have developed their own materials. Now, based on the individualized catechesis method, the *Adaptive Finding God Program* includes catechetical instruction for teen faith mentors to follow, as well as a variety of hands-on learning tools, including puzzles, concept stories, and songs.

It's important to have a good supply of materials necessary for this kind of teaching on hand—construction paper, colored pencils, markers, crayons, and the like. You will also need to provide the supplies for craft projects—scissors, paste, tape, and so forth. Mentors often bring supplies from home, although they shouldn't be expected to do this. As the program begins in the fall, it is critical to observe how your teen faith mentors are adapting the lessons so you can provide the necessary materials.

Recruiting Teen Faith Mentors

One of your most important and critical duties—and one of the biggest challenges—is recruiting and training talented and committed teen faith mentors. This is a constant task. You will need more mentors as your program grows, and mentors who move on in their lives will need to be replaced every year. Recruitment is easier when your parish is welcoming to people with disabilities, when they are visible in your parish, and when parishioners are frequently reminded about the successes in the program and the ongoing needs of their fellow parishioners.

A direct appeal is usually effective. I preach regularly at Our Lady of Grace, and a couple of times a year I invite teens to consider becoming faith mentors in the program. I invite young people to talk to me after Mass and to observe a lesson; people always do.

I have had great success recruiting at local high schools, both Catholic and public. Many high schools require students to complete some hours of community service. Also, students are often looking for community-service opportunities to strengthen their college applications. Some high school students are considering careers in special education and are looking for experience in the field. I ask high school guidance counselors to send me students who might be interested. As a professional in the field, I'm often invited to speak about developmental disabilities at high schools and at parent meetings; when I do, I always mention the needs of children with autism and the need for teen mentors. Perhaps people in your parish who are professionals can do the same when they talk to community groups.

Some of the best recruiters are the mentors themselves. Many come to the program because a friend has told them how rewarding it is to help a child with disabilities receive the sacraments and develop a relationship with God. I always ask interested teens to bring a friend along to informational meetings, and most of them do. Teenagers are intensely social. Teaching in the adaptive religious education program is something productive and interesting that friends can do together. The program is a place where they can make new friends. Some mentors have even recruited their younger brothers and sisters into the program.

Many faith mentors have had personal contact with a child with disabilities before they come to the program. One of our excellent faith mentors is Gary, the brother of a boy with autism. He came reluctantly at first; his parents prodded him. But after a few weeks he developed a close bond with his student. One morning the student, a small boy, clung to Gary's leg and could hardly be persuaded to let go. Gary was disarmed by the boy's devotion. He liked the feeling of being loved; he liked the idea that he really had something important to offer to someone who needed him.

Another source of faith mentors is the program itself. One of our mentors is Adam, a fourteen-year-old boy with autism who was confirmed after four years in the program. Usually, students leave the program after being confirmed, but Adam wanted to stay on. I paired him with an experienced mentor, and the two of them worked with a young boy who was preparing to receive the Eucharist. The boy connected strongly with Adam. This thrilled Adam, who was very pleased to be able to offer himself to another person.

That's not unusual. The program has a powerful, positive impact on many teen mentors, who, after all, are struggling with the worries and uncertainties of adolescence themselves.

Working with Parents

The program frequently has a positive impact on parents that goes beyond the satisfaction of seeing their children learn about God and receiving the sacraments. Many parents are drawn into a deeper faith life through the program. Some reconnect with the Church after a long period of alienation, hurt, and indifference. Some become active Catholics for the first time. The program is a source of personal support for parents; they are able to talk about their stressful lives in an atmosphere of honesty, mutual understanding, and support.

Five reasons parents are central to the success of the Individualized Catechesis Method

1. Parents help teen mentors get to know their children, their strengths, likes and dislikes, and learning styles.
2. Sometimes a child's anxiety in a new situation is eased by a parent's presence.
3. Parents need to reinforce lessons during the week.
4. Parents need to see their child learn from a teen faith mentor.
5. Parents have their own facilitated discussion during class.

First, you must make contact with parents. Some will make their needs known to parish ministers, but many won't. Many parents don't think their children are eligible for religious education because the parish doesn't supply the kind of support services they are used to receiving in public schools. Often, parents think that religious education is too hard for their children. They don't want their children to be in a situation in which they will fail. Perhaps for this reason, many parents tend to underestimate their child's abilities, especially when the child is young. In my professional work, I have often seen young people perform much better than expected when they have the opportunity to express themselves and when adults are patient with them.

Parents are required to attend the program with their children for several reasons. One is quite practical: it's crucial that mentors get to know the child well, and no one knows a child better than his or her parents. The mentor must understand how the child learns, what's upsetting to the child, what he or she likes, and the strategies that parents use to encourage and reward the child. Having parents involved from the beginning and present for class greatly enhances this communication. Sometimes an anxious child who is new to the program will want the parent to sit in on the lesson.

Parents also need to attend because we ask them to reinforce the lesson at home at least once during the week. Many children need the extra instruction because they don't grasp the full lesson the first time. At the end of each Sunday class, the teen faith mentor meets briefly with the parent to review the lesson. Parental involvement of this kind is desirable in all religious education. Fortunately, we have good reasons for requiring their presence in the adaptive religious education program, and their presence benefits everyone.

I also like parents to be present so that they can see their child learn. Many are skeptical when they're told that a teenager will mentor their child. Many have seen little more than failure and disappointment when it comes to their child learning. Some don't know what their child is capable of doing. Many parents are astonished at the progress their child makes during a forty-five-minute class once a week.

The final reason for asking parents to attend is to bring them together for a facilitated discussion while their children are having their lessons. As the program coordinator, I led this discussion myself for several years before passing the baton to another facilitator. Many topics come up in these discussions. Parents talk about how difficult their home life is with a child with disabilities. Sometimes they talk about their difficulties in church. They share ideas. They tell one another about services that are available for their children. Often families develop relationships with one another, which both helps the children who can have trouble making friends and breaks down the isolation that so often afflicts their parents.

Working with Faith Mentors and Students

The success of the program depends on the relationship between the teen faith mentor and the student. The program coordinator's most important job is making sure that this relationship is working well. The coordinator must match students with the mentor who is best able to teach them. To do this, the coordinator must understand how each student learns and how individual mentors teach.

One of the biggest lessons I learned in the first year of the program was the importance of understanding how students learn. Four children were preparing to receive the Eucharist; each of them behaved and communicated very differently, and each was successfully taught in different ways.

> **Freddy** was a boy with a high-functioning form of autism. He understood language very well, and he loved to play word games. He liked to distract his mentor from the lesson by posing riddles.
>
> **Benjamin** didn't speak much, and it took him a long time to process information. He learned by doing and seeing rather than by listening to the mentor explain the lesson. He loved crafts. That first year he made an Advent wreath out of colored construction paper. He took my hand, pushed it to the yellow paper flame and said, "Hot."
>
> **James** had a hard time staying focused on a topic. His attention would wander, but he would eventually return to the topic of his pet dog. He loved his dog and carried a picture of him in his pocket whenever he left home.
>
> **Keith** was an extremely logical and concrete thinker. He understood that Jesus is the man who is depicted on the crucifix, but he did not understand how the same Jesus could be in a piece of bread. He said, "How can Jesus be up there [on the crucifix] and in this [holding the unconsecrated host we were using for practice]?"

I worked with mentors to find the teaching style best suited to help these boys learn. For Freddy, who was verbally adept, I found a mentor who was skilled at explaining and visually illustrating concepts, taking advantage of his good expressive language. (I also helped her avoid getting caught up in his riddles.) I matched Benjamin with a mentor who loved craft projects. When James's mentor noticed his obsession with his dog, she made up stories with a religious lesson in which a dog (which had the same name as James's dog) played an important role. James would listen to the stories intently, waiting for his dog to appear.

For Keith, I got involved myself. (In fact, his mentor came to me and said, "Deacon, you're going to have to answer this one.") Keith wanted a logical explanation for how the same Jesus who was on the cross could also be present in the host. I explained the consecration of the bread and wine as best I could, and I also told him that we can't "prove" many things about the mysteries of our faith in the same way that we can prove things with numbers. Keith accepted that, but years later, he's still puzzled. Whenever I see him, he wants to talk about the Real Presence of Jesus.

Keith's story is particularly relevant for catechists. Many children with autism are logical and concrete thinkers (though usually not in as extreme a way as Keith is). They don't grasp nuance and subtleties, and they dislike ambiguity. For them, it's important that material be well organized and presented in a logical way that leads to a conclusion. Many truths and mysteries of our faith don't fit neatly into this pedagogical model. Catechists who teach children with autism and other special needs need to adjust their teaching methods accordingly. I frequently remind mentors that they will never "prove" some things about our faith. If they keep trying, they will be frustrated.

Like the children they teach, mentors have their own special strengths. Some make up good stories; others are skilled at craft projects. Some teach with music; still others are good at designing games. I try to expose mentors to different teaching techniques so they can add new methods to their repertoire.

Learning to Communicate

Faith mentors need to learn how to communicate with their students. To do this, mentors must know about the characteristics of autism that most affect communication. I talk to faith mentors about this at the orientation workshop before class begins, and I continue to work on it throughout the year. The following are some of the most important points to understand.

Learn to wait. Many children with autism respond slowly. Most of us enter the ebb and flow of conversation naturally. Someone asks a question, and we answer. Someone makes a comment, and we make one of our own. Many children with autism can't do this because their ability to process information is impaired. They can respond appropriately but only after a long pause. The pause can be as long as ninety seconds in some cases. Ten or fifteen seconds is a long time to wait for an answer to a question. Ninety seconds seems like an eternity.

When interacting with a person with autism for the first time, people are usually disturbed by this delayed response. I have been working professionally with children with autism for many years, and I still have to remind myself to wait for answers to my questions. More often than not, children will come up with the answer, but I have to be patient and wait for it. The latent response can also be disturbing to children with autism. They are aware that they are expected to respond more quickly to questions or to new information, but they simply can't do it. This is one reason why children with autism often talk endlessly about the Civil War, automobiles, baseball team rosters, and other topics that they've studied to the point of obsession. It gives them something to talk about when they're in anxiety-producing situations with other people.

Create a calm setting for auditory processing. People with autism typically have difficulty sorting out information from the various sounds they hear. They don't hear what you're hearing. You might be able to read a book while music is playing softly in the background or carry on a conversation while watching television. By and large, people with autism can't push extraneous noise into the background to focus on what you are saying. This is why group singing, story time, and other group activities in organized academic-like settings often don't work well with these children. That's why classrooms for individualized catechesis need to be quiet places.

Allow for adjustment time. People with autism typically need time to get adjusted to new situations, even those that they've encountered before, like Mass and school. They can usually do it, but they need time. A new setting (like the church or school) and new people (the priest, mentor, and other children) bring a flood of sights, sounds, and other sensory data that need to be sorted out and understood. Faith mentors (and others) can ease this transition by moving into new material slowly.

One of the most noticeable impairments of autism is the inability to make small talk. Small talk—chatting about the weather and insignificant events of the day—helps us ease into new situations.

For people with autism, small talk does not make sense. Instead of trying to make small talk, mentors can usually put students at ease by talking about their preferred topic.

Stay concrete and literal. Much of our language is metaphorical. We like puns, proverbs, adages, analogies. People with autism tend to think concretely and literally. Idioms like "this place is a madhouse" and "hit the nail on the head" can seem absurd and confusing. For them, words have one meaning. They often don't get jokes. Humor that depends on wordplay, misunderstandings, and thwarted plans will be lost on them. What seems like affectionate banter to us might seem like bullying to a child who is a concrete thinker and who often really has been bullied by other children.

Accept bad days with humor and compassion. Children with autism are easily thrown off kilter. Bad days are caused by problems that seem small and ordinary to others—a snowstorm, not enough sleep, hunger, a spat with a sibling. A child might arrive at class angry and distressed because he didn't get enough sleep or because his mother drove a different route than the one he's accustomed to. Some days are just bad days; the mentor needs to accept that not much will get done on those days. It's important that mentors and parents be in good communication about this.

Learning Moments for Teen Faith Mentors

I explain autism to faith mentors in an orientation session on a Saturday before classes begin. I talk for about three hours, and we provide lunch. New mentors are required to attend; returning faith mentors are invited, as are all the mentors' parents. This orientation should be given by a knowledgeable person, usually someone who works in the field of autism and special education. These people are not hard to find; there are surely special education professionals in your community and perhaps in your parish. Most of them are accustomed to explaining disabilities to nonprofessionals.

While we prepare faith mentors the best we can, there's no substitute for on-the-job experience. I find that I'm best able to help them when "learning moments" arise.

One such moment happens when the mentor sees stimming in action for the first time. I talk about stimming in the orientation, but most mentors don't really understand what it is until they see a child flapping his hands in class. Then I help them see it for what it is—a reaction to stress, happiness or excitement, sensory overload, or boredom.

Tantrums and meltdowns are also learning moments. When a child gets upset in class for the first time, most mentors get upset, too. They assume that either they or the student has done something wrong and that something must be done immediately to settle things down. But no one is to blame for meltdowns. They happen because something has upset a child who often lacks the verbal facility to say why. Sometimes the only thing to do is to let a tantrum run its course and then help the faith mentor find a way to allow the student to continue and finish the lesson if possible.

Very often I urge mentors to let students dictate some of the rules. Children with autism often cope with new and anxiety-producing situations by trying to control them, at least in part. Usually, it's better to work patiently with these rules than oppose them. I tell mentors about Jim, a boy who is now in his fourth year of the adaptive religious education program. When he first came in, Jim insisted that his mother sit with him during the lessons. After a while he decided that his mother's presence wasn't necessary, but he wanted to be alone with his mentor in the classroom. Everything would go well until someone else came into the room; then Jim would fly into a rage. Gradually, Jim relaxed his rules. He's now comfortable with the people in the program, and he is making good progress toward Confirmation.

Being Comfortable with Uncertainty

Successful faith mentors have to get used to uncertainty. It's hard to know what a child with autism knows. It's hard to understand the behavior of children with autism. They give their teachers less feedback than most children do. It's difficult to understand why things go wrong and why things go right. Often, a student will suddenly do something that he'd been refusing to do. You don't have to know why something went wrong; just be prepared to move to plan B.

All teachers wonder what they have communicated to their students. Faith mentors in the adaptive religious education program experience this uncertainty acutely. Often, the best mentoring and teaching means letting things unfold in their own way.

I think of Robert, a young man with cerebral palsy and a hearing impairment. He does not speak very much; he may have autism as well, but it's hard to tell. Despite his severe impairments, Robert is very charismatic and he connects very deeply with some people. Faith mentors who understand Robert have been able to accomplish remarkable things with him. They engage in back-and-forth discussions with him, with Robert using a special communications device. At times Robert can be very animated in his interactions with mentors, something that his parents and therapists don't often see. I haven't been directly involved as much with teaching Robert. I stepped back and watched the teen mentors try different techniques until something worked.

The mentors have communicated the core truths of our faith to Robert. I think Robert grasps them, but, as is often the case, it's difficult to know precisely what he knows. I tell mentors to do their best and trust the Holy Spirit. As Saint Ignatius of Loyola put it, "Make a competent and sufficient effort, and leave the rest to God."

> As Saint Ignatius of Loyola put it, "Make a competent and sufficient effort, and leave the rest to God."

7

Sacraments

Sacraments are at the heart of Catholic life, so it's no surprise that learning about the sacraments and preparing children to receive the sacraments is a major part of the adaptive religious education program. Often, young people come into the program because their parents want them to receive First Eucharist and Reconciliation. Students complete the program by receiving the Sacrament of Confirmation.

The first challenge is to establish the fact that children with disabilities can receive the sacraments. Baptism is seldom an issue, but many Catholics, including some pastoral leaders, mistakenly believe that children with disabilities don't need the Eucharist, Reconciliation, and Confirmation, or that these children can't meet the minimal requirements for receiving them. Sometimes it is said that they are in a separate spiritual category—"God's special children"—and don't need the sacramental graces available to other Catholics. I started our program to challenge just such an assumption when the two boys with autism were denied First Eucharist.

Some pastoral leaders and parents have honest doubts about the ability of children with autism and other disabilities to grasp the meaning of the sacraments with sufficient depth to receive them. These misgivings are almost always unfounded. According to the USCCB, all that's necessary to receive First Eucharist is for "the person to be able to distinguish the Body of Christ from ordinary food, even if this recognition is evidenced through manner, gesture, or reverential silence rather than verbally." According to the guidelines, all that's necessary for a person to receive Reconciliation is a "sense of contrition . . . even if he or she cannot describe the sin precisely in words, the person may receive sacramental absolution." And the USCCB guidelines state that baptized Catholics "who properly and reasonably request" the Sacrament of Confirmation can receive it if they are "suitably instructed, properly disposed, and able to renew their baptismal promises." The guidelines continue, however: "Persons who because of developmental or mental disabilities may never attain the use of reason are to be encouraged either directly or, if necessary, through their parents or guardian to receive the sacrament of confirmation at the appropriate time." Virtually all children with developmental disabilities are capable of preparing to meet these criteria.

That doesn't mean that sacramental preparation is without its challenges. It takes work, considerable creativity, persistence, and acute judgment. Most children with autism are concrete thinkers. They're drawn to the outward signs of the sacraments—water, bread, wine, oil. But understanding the spiritual truths that these signs signify often comes more slowly. Even though the requirements for receiving these sacraments are few, we are still charged with preparing children as well as possible. Many parishes have developed ways to prepare them, and Loyola Press offers adaptive sacramental preparation kits for First Eucharist, Reconciliation, and Confirmation for children with autism and other special needs in both English and Spanish.

Baptism

Baptism is seldom an issue because most children with autism are baptized as infants or toddlers, long before their disability becomes apparent and is diagnosed. Just to be clear, canon law states that disability itself is never a reason for refusing or deferring Baptism. Anyone who asks for Baptism can receive the sacrament. People who lack the use of reason are to be baptized if a parent or guardian asks. The only reason for denying someone Baptism is when there is no hope that he or she will be raised as a Catholic.

The Baptism of a disabled adult may occasionally come up. This has happened once in my parish's program. An unbaptized man in his early twenties, severely impaired with autism, approached me with his mother asking to be baptized. He was attracted to the Church by the example of the Catholic caregivers at the group home in which he lived. We prepared him for Baptism using the materials that are part of the curriculum for all students. These materials focus on what the sacramentals used in Baptism signify. The water brings new life; the oil anoints the person as God's special child; the candle signifies the light of Christ bringing wisdom. Faith mentors include the parents in this lesson when they can. Parents bring photos of the child's Baptism, and these are incorporated into the lesson.

When I do Baptisms in my parish, I always include children as much as possible. I invite all the children to the baptismal font to help me. Children hold the book for me, carry the precious oils, and surround me as I pour the water of Baptism on the baby's head. It's a joyous occasion, something I recall when some of the children I baptized come into the adaptive religious education program as students.

Jerry is one of these children. I remember him well because he was one of a set of triplets baptized on a beautiful Sunday afternoon. I remember the beaming faces of Jerry's parents and grandparents as I baptized the three babies. Four years later, Jerry's mother approached me after Mass looking drawn and grief stricken. She started to tell me what was wrong, but she broke down, and Jerry's grandmother had to tell me the story: Jerry had been diagnosed with autism. He appeared to be severely afflicted. The four-year-old had no language, and he spent his time in motion around the house and waving his hand in front of his eyes in constant stimming. Jerry's mother was crushed. Like all parents of children with developmental disabilities, Jerry's mother had to radically adjust her expectations for her child. Seeing Jerry receive the sacraments was one of the dreams she thought she had to give up.

But Jerry came into the program, and he's made good progress in his preparation for First Eucharist. His mother and grandmother help in the program. Two teen faith mentors work with Jerry. He's learning about God and coming to understand how God comes to us in the bread of Holy Communion. As I watch Jerry work, I sometimes recall the joyous day of his Baptism. Baptism was the beginning of Jerry's sacramental life, not the end.

The Eucharist

The Eucharist is "the summit and the source of all Christian worship and life," as canon law eloquently states. It's fair to say that the Eucharist is the summit of the adaptive religious education program as well. It's the central sacrament, and we devote a lot of time and attention to it.

Again, the USCCB guidelines state that the only criterion for reception of Holy Communion is the same for everyone—"that the person be able to distinguish the Body of Christ from ordinary food." This recognition can be demonstrated by "manner, gesture, or reverential silence." When in doubt, pastoral ministers are to decide in favor of "the right of the baptized person to receive the sacrament." Clearly, almost every baptized Catholic can and should receive Holy Communion.

Our goal is not just to meet these minimum standards but to bring each child to the deepest appreciation of the Eucharist that he or she is capable of. It's often difficult to know when or whether we've achieved this goal. It's often hard to know what these children know. I tell the teen faith mentors not to be surprised at anything when they start preparing children for the Eucharist. The notion that God comes to us in the form of Holy Communion bread is not an easy concept for children with autism to grasp. They think logically and concretely; metaphors and analogies are confusing; abstract concepts, hints, suggestions, and insights are often out of their reach.

In teaching them about the Eucharist, we need to be creative and persistent. It's important for the children to practice. They need to touch and handle the unconsecrated host. We also invite them to eat the host and taste the unconsecrated wine. Be prepared for surprising reactions. During our first year, we practiced receiving the Precious Blood from the chalice. I filled the chalice with unconsecrated communion wine, lined up the children, and invited them to taste it. One boy immediately spat it out on the floor; he was expecting the taste of red soda. Some children don't like the taste of unleavened bread and refuse to eat it. The bread and wine of Holy Communion may infringe on the strict rules about food that many children with autism have, so techniques such as food chaining may be required to help the child consume the host. Food chaining is a technique used by occupational therapists to transition children from foods that they know and like to foods that are unfamiliar. Changes are minute and typically involve a change to taste, temperature, or texture. Working from a flavor and texture that a child enjoys to one that may be challenging can take patience and time; increasing the variety or amount of food can take months, or even years.

Scott, a child who was at a point in his religious education where he was ready to receive Holy Communion at Mass, would not touch it or go near anyone who distributed it. Very subtly we introduced an unconsecrated host. Formal chaining began with his looking at the host, kissing the host, and taking a small nibble from one. Finally, he took a large bite and swallowed it. This has taken months, but he has made excellent progress and has now received First Eucharist.

Often, an individual child's rules about food are hard to understand. Children with autism often have different rules for different places; for example, they might eat foods at school that they would never eat at home. Rules change without explanation. I think of Richard, who entered preparation for First Eucharist with great reluctance. Although he appeared to understand that the host at Mass was different from regular food, he was afraid of the host; he watched warily from across the room while the others practiced receiving it. Over time he gradually came nearer and eventually touched the host and tasted it, but then suddenly he withdrew and would have nothing to do with it. This went on for several years. Then one Sunday, quite unexpectedly, he went into the Communion procession with his mother, bowed in front of the Eucharistic minister, received the host in his hand, said "Amen," and consumed it. Richard has been receiving Holy Communion ever since.

I don't know why Richard behaved the way he did. I don't know why he was afraid or why he abruptly decided that Holy Communion was safe. Richard may not know himself. "Why?" is a question you will often ask when working with children with autism. Often, there is no good answer. Rules help children with autism cope with situations that distress them, and there's no question that the continual challenges involved in schooling can be upsetting. It's important to be patient with rules and adapt to a child's puzzling behavior. Eventually, understanding will come. The Holy Spirit finds a way.

Stories are usually effective in teaching about the Eucharist. The teen faith mentors will tell the story of the Last Supper and compare it to supper with their family at home. The mentors will describe the miracle of the loaves and fish. They will help the child draw pictures of these events. I tell mentors to avoid extensive verbal explanation, and

I advise them never to try to persuade a child that the Communion bread is the Body of Christ. Explanations are almost always confusing, and elaborate discussions are usually counterproductive. Stories, pictures, and practicing Communion yield better results. Practice in class is supplemented by carefully observing Communion during Mass. The children are unsettled by unfamiliar and "strange" things, and for most of them, the Eucharist falls into the "strange" category. Practice and repetition make the rite familiar and remove the anxiety and distress.

Persistence is a virtue in an adaptive religious education program. One boy I worked with, Steve, was a very concrete thinker and could not understand how the ordinary Communion bread could become the Body of Christ. This was a sticking point that became an obstacle to his receiving Holy Communion. I tried many ways to explain it. Finally, I began to go to Mass with Steve. At the moment of consecration, I would tell him, "There. That is when the change happens." For some reason, this satisfied Steve. Knowing when the change occurred satisfied his need for specificity, and he accepted the miracle of transubstantiation.

You will likely have children in the program who are following gluten-free diets because it is thought that this can sometimes reduce symptoms of autism and improve cognitive functioning. You may also have children with celiac disease and other conditions that require a gluten-free diet. For some time, Catholics with these allergies have been able to receive Holy Communion in the form of hosts with a miniscule amount of gluten. Most parishes are accustomed to the protocol for using these low-gluten hosts at Mass. You will have to follow the same protocol when practicing Communion with children on gluten-free diets. These are the rules for handling low-gluten hosts, consecrated and umconsecrated:

- The low-gluten host must never come in contact with typical hosts.

- The low-gluten host must be kept in a separate ciborium both before and after consecration.
- The Eucharistic minister who administers the low-gluten host should never touch a gluten host. If by necessity, the celebrant is the only minister present, he should wear a glove so as to protect the recipient from any exposure from the gluten hosts handled earlier by the minister.

Reconciliation

The Sacrament of Penance and Reconciliation is received in tandem with the Eucharist. Our usual practice is for children to celebrate Reconciliation first and receive the Eucharist soon after.

Again, the USCCB guidelines state that people with disabilities can receive sacramental absolution as long as they have a sense of contrition for having committed sin. Like the requirement for receiving the Eucharist—that the person be able to distinguish the bread of Holy Communion from ordinary food—this is a minimal standard that encompasses almost every baptized Catholic. As with the Eucharist, we try to bring the child to the fullest appreciation of the Sacrament of Penance and Reconciliation that he or she is capable of.

The challenges of preparing these children for the sacrament boil down to three questions:

1. Does the child know right from wrong?
2. How can the child express contrition?
3. How can a child with limited verbal skills (or none at all) communicate with the priest?

Jerry, the triplet child I mentioned earlier, illustrates these challenges in their most acute form. Because Jerry could speak only a few words when he came into the program, he challenged us to think creatively about how to prepare him for a sacrament that ordinarily depends on verbal communication.

The first task was to help Jerry tell right from wrong. It was difficult to judge how much he knew about this. Although he didn't speak, Jerry often responded when spoken to and seemed to understand many words. Like many children with autism, he gave the impression of knowing more than he let on, but it was impossible to know for sure. We kept things simple. We asked Jerry's mother and grandmother to tell us about things he did at home that were helpful and unhelpful. Jerry's mentors then drew pictures on index cards illustrating these things—for example, fighting with his sisters and putting his plate in the sink after dinner. The mentor played a game of flash cards with Jerry. She showed him a card; he placed it in the "right" or "wrong" pile. In this way Jerry was able to show us that he understood what good behavior is. Our pastor then observed the teen mentor as she used the cards (thus teaching him how to communicate with Jerry) and successfully administered the sacrament to Jerry.

We use variations of this technique for many children in the program. The idea is for parents to identify behaviors at home that the child can understand—things they actually do—and then devise a visual way to present it. This also makes it easier for our priest to understand how to communicate with nonverbal children. Faith mentors sometimes encounter resistance from parents who don't think their child can do anything wrong in a moral sense because of their disability. This question needs to be asked, but our general feeling is that children in an adaptive religious education program can understand, even in a small way, good behavior and bad behavior and can express remorse. In this way, they can receive the healing and grace of God's forgiveness.

The final task is the administration of the sacrament itself. Receiving Reconciliation means that the child must meet with the priest, which is something new and different, the kind of thing that tends to upset children with autism. We make sure that the priest has visited class often enough not to be a stranger. In most cases, the mentor will explain to the priest how the child communicates, what might upset him or her, and anything else that might affect their communication. Watching teen mentors explain these subtle issues to the priest is one of the delights of the adaptive religious education program.

Confirmation

Confirmation is the last of the Sacraments of Initiation—the sacrament by which a Catholic becomes a full adult member of the Church.

We want every student in the program to be confirmed. This goal surprises some people. They assume that Confirmation is out of reach for children with autism or other disabilities because their disabilities are permanent and often severe, making full Christian maturity impossible. But who among us is "fully mature"? The goal for children with autism and other disabilities is the same as it is for everyone—the greatest degree of maturity of which they are capable.

The USCCB guidelines for Confirmation underscore this point. Clearly—as with the Eucharist and Reconciliation—the Church's attitude toward the sacrament is broad and inclusive. Sacramental graces are for everyone.

In the adaptive religious education program, preparation for Confirmation is an individual matter. We begin to consider the sacrament when the student is twelve or thirteen—the usual age for the sacrament—but there is no rush for it. The aim of preparation is to help the student achieve the fullest degree of maturity he or she is capable of at the time. Maturity is not a static condition for children with autism (or for anyone). The child's faith will grow and deepen over time, as will his or her participation in the life of the Church. The decision to present someone for Confirmation involves a subjective judgment about the child's readiness.

Confirmation preparation emphasizes several themes. One is helping the student achieve a deeper sense of belonging to the larger Church. Instruction includes lessons on the global scope of the Church, its history, and its structure. We encourage students to attend Mass regularly and to participate in other parish activities. We help candidates for Confirmation achieve a sense of responsibility for their participation in the Church. Growing in maturity also means being able to take action on one's own without needing to be told what to do. Finally, preparation emphasizes service. We talk about ways to help other people and to find ways to serve in the Church.

Serving others is especially important and a special challenge. Self-centeredness, a problem for all of us, is an especially strong inclination for people with autism. Everyone who struggles with a disability expends much time and energy meeting his or her own needs. Again, autism and some other disabilities actually impair a person's ability to recognize other people as individuals with unique identities. Most children need to understand how they can serve others.

Considering the needs of others did not come naturally to Chris, an eighth grader with autism who came into our program to be prepared for Confirmation. Chris was a bright boy who loved to read. He understood God and the basics of the Gospel, and he knew the difference between right and wrong. But Chris seemed entirely focused on himself. He had no friends. Like many children with autism, he rarely acknowledged other people. He was content to do his own thing, and he didn't seem to understand that other people had thoughts, feelings, and needs that were different from his own.

Chris's mentor was a teen who was very active in the parish. He talked to Chris about his youth group, his Scout troop, and serving as an usher at Mass. Chris began to act as one of the Eucharistic ministers in our practice sessions with unconsecrated hosts. Then the faith mentor brought Chris together with Jason, a younger boy in the class who had no verbal skills.

Jason liked Chris. They began to sit together before and after class. One day Chris picked up the book *Winnie the Pooh* and began to read. Jason looked up, smiled, and then began to laugh. The more Chris read, the harder Jason laughed. Jason laughed so hard he fell off his chair. Since then, Jason and Chris have developed a close relationship. Chris was confirmed, but he didn't leave the program. He has stayed on as an assistant faith mentor, working primarily with his friend Jason.

This sounds like a small thing. But for a boy with severe autism, it's a big thing. Chris is being transformed from a boy confined to the prison of the self to an adult Catholic who is attuned to other people, interested in their well-being, and willing and able to help them. It's a miracle of grace—the grace of the sacraments—which are meant for all.

8

Surprises

Several things about our individualized catechesis program have surprised me. Some are things I observed, and others are conclusions I drew after reflecting on six years of experience.

First, here are some things I observed. I had a hunch that teenagers would make effective mentors, but I was surprised at just how good they were. They dedicated themselves to the work. They got attached to their students very quickly. They "got" their students. Understanding the child is a crucial and elusive skill. Those who communicate well with children with autism must discover what interests them and how they communicate. Teenagers are very good at this—better than I thought they would be.

I was surprised and pleased at how creative the teen mentors were. They would take a lesson plan and figure out a way to communicate the ideas in it using words, pictures, stories, games, puzzles, songs—whatever helped their student understand it. Teen mentors aren't attached to one way of teaching. They are more adept at visual, nonverbal methods than most adults, which is essential for the many children whose word and language abilities are impaired.

I have observed some collateral benefits to having teen mentors which don't directly relate to religious education. The teens enjoy being with one another on Sunday mornings. They joke and mingle before and after class. They make friends with one another. It is an opportunity for young men and women to be together in an emotionally safe place.

I have also watched some of the older students carefully observing how their faith mentors interact with one another. They imitate what they see their teachers doing. Most young people with autism need to learn appropriate social behavior. Their teen faith mentors not only teach them about God, but they also teach them how to be typical teenagers.

I am surprised and pleased at the way parents and families have benefited from the program. Few religious education programs require parents to attend with their children; we felt we could require it for practical reasons. Children are usually more secure with their parents around, and parents are able to help mentors understand their child. But the parents benefited personally as well. The facilitated discussion gave them an opportunity to share their frustrations and their hopes and successes. Some parents made friends with one another. For some, the Sunday-morning classes began a process of reconnecting with the Catholic Church.

My final observation has to do with the surprising degree of success the program has had. I'm not surprised that the program has worked; I'm surprised at how well it has worked. Every child who has stayed with the program has received the sacraments. We have found a way to communicate the essential truths of the Gospel to children with a wide array of sensory, intellectual, and social impairments. I was surprised to see some of the older students becoming faith mentors after they were confirmed. Some of our older students with autism have been accepted into academically competitive Catholic high schools. I think the program can take some credit for instilling the self-confidence necessary for a young person with disabilities to do something like that. I am also pleased that a number of our mentors have gone on to prepare for careers in special education, psychology, or medicine.

After reflecting on my experience and observations, I've reached certain conclusions that may be of help to you as you consider starting a program yourself.

First, young people are capable of more than you think. This is true of both students and mentors. Children with autism can learn more than most people think they can. All they need is the opportunity, sufficient communication, and teachers who don't have low expectations of what children can do. Teenagers make fine mentors; some are extraordinarily creative and effective. This surprises many people. That only proves my point: teens can do more than we think. Like their students, all they need is the opportunity and encouragement from elders who don't have fixed ideas about the capabilities of adolescents.

Second, this is religious education—something that all parishes do, and something that all parents do if they desire an active life of faith for their children. Children with autism and other special needs present a particular set of challenges, but these are challenges that mentors and catechetical leaders can rise to. Teenagers can learn how to teach the faith to children with autism and other developmental disabilities.

This leads to the question of professional expertise. An experienced religious educator with an open mind and a flair for working with teenagers can run your program. People like that can probably be found in your parish; if not, they can be found in the parish next door. You do need to draw on the expertise of professionals in order to understand children's disabilities, but you can find these professionals in your parish and in your community. Materials are being developed specifically for children with autism and other special needs; the *Adaptive Finding God Program* uses teen mentors, as well as learning tools, to make the *Catechism* concrete and teachable.

One of the lessons I've learned as a professional is not to overthink my role. The aura of professional expertise can hinder good practice instead of enhancing it. Often, the best course is to let the child, teen, or adult with a developmental disability guide me in the right direction, and to be confident enough to do that, I need to know the person well.

And that's my final point—the essential thing is relationship. Religious education is about cultivating a relationship with God through Jesus Christ and the power of the Holy Spirit. The way to help children with autism and other disabilities do this is through building a relationship with them. That's what an individualized catechesis method can help you do—essentially convey God's love.

Epilogue

The program described in this book took several years to develop. The 2006 pilot program at Our Lady of Grace parish didn't even have a name. It consisted of me, five boys with autism, and some teenagers learning to be faith mentors. We succeeded, the program grew, and we got better at teaching and learning. I helped other parishes start similar programs and described the program at conferences and workshops. Then national organizations became interested. It seemed to me and to others in the field that we had a model that many parishes could follow to provide religious education to children with autism and other disabilities.

We took a giant step toward realizing this vision when Loyola Press entered the picture in 2012. Loyola Press, which has been developing and publishing religious education curricula for decades, wanted to serve students with disabilities. They learned about the program at Our Lady of Grace, liked what they saw, and proposed that we work together to adapt their *Finding God* curriculum. This is what we've done, and the result is the *Adaptive Finding God Program*—a full-fledged religious education program that can be used successfully with children with autism and other special needs.

This program overcomes the biggest obstacle faced by parishes that want to serve children with autism and other disabilities and parents who desperately want to find ways to share God with their children: the hurdle of developing a program more or less from scratch. The *Adaptive Finding God Program* has all the materials needed to implement an individualized catechesis method in any parish. It includes core catechetical content aligned with an existing curriculum, leveled instruction, training materials for teen faith mentors, learning tools, and other materials that program coordinators and mentors need. Parishes can take this program and make it their own.

For generations, Catholics with disabilities and their families have been underserved by their Church. The success of an individualized catechesis method and the development of the *Adaptive Finding God Program* are signs that things are changing. At long last, pastors, catechetical leaders, and families have the tools they need to bring the graces of the sacraments and the fullness of faith to children with autism and other special needs.

Many obstacles remain. Leaders at all levels of the Church have much work to do to bring all Catholics into full participation in parish life. But in one area at least—religious education—we have a clear path forward. I invite you to join me on it.

Acknowledgments

In preparing this book, I received a great deal of assistance, inspiration, and support from many sources.

I am grateful to Grace Harding, Sister Michelle Grgurich, and Eleanor Marshall of the Office of Disabilities of the Diocese of Pittsburgh for listening to my initial laments over the injustice suffered by those two young boys that started me on this journey. And to Father Richard Infante—I wonder if any other priest would have had the vision and trust to allow such a venture to move forward—without your support and counsel, I don't think I could have proceeded. To the children in the program over these years, their parents, and all those wonderful teen faith mentors who spent hours in our Sunday-morning classes, I am very grateful. I am grateful as well to Lindsay Pfister and the teachers at Our Lady of Grace School for their support and assistance.

In this journey I've met holy people who have provided guidance, thought, support, and direct assistance: Cardinal Donald Wuerl; Cardinal Daniel DiNardo from the Archdiocese of Galveston-Houston, who grew up some three miles from my home; Bishop Robert Donnelly of the Diocese of Toledo; Bishop David Zubik of Pittsburgh, who from my first application interview into the deaconate program has challenged me to respond and serve with the gifts God has given me; Father William Byrne; and Sargent Shriver and Mark Shriver. To Lisa Martinelli for your support, courage, and enthusiasm in demonstrating that this method could be successful in another parish. To my fellow board members at the National Apostolate for Inclusion Ministry, especially Bishop Mitchell Rozanski of Baltimore. Father Enzo Addari, Bill Fleming, Deacon Jim Lavin, Judy Sunder and Ted Sunder, Father Joe McNulty, Dennis McNulty, Helaine Arnold, Deacon Ray Daull, and Barbara Lampe. At the National Catholic Partnership on Disability, I have been blessed to receive the assistance of Janice Benton and Martin Benton, as well as Nancy Thompson and the Autism Task Force. To the Sisters of Charity and the DePaul Institute, who during my diaconate formation showed and taught me that it is children first and disability second, thank you.

In a fundamental way, I am so grateful to Joellyn Cicciarelli, Maria Mondragón, and Tom McGrath at Loyola Press for the trust, vision, and courage to give me a chance. And to Jim Manney, who helped me transform my thoughts, words, and passions into this wonderful book.

Finally, there are some people who have provided support because it was a good thing to do, and to them I'm eternally grateful—Peg Kolm; Mary O'Meara; and most especially my wife, Nancy, and our sons, Dan, Brian, and Mark, who participated in all our trips and adventures as the first peer models for my students with autism.

About the Author

Larry Sutton is an ordained deacon and a psychologist specializing in autism. He is the former director of the Western Pennsylvania Office of Autism Services and is currently the Director of the Pre-Theology program at St. Vincent College. He is nationally recognized for developing his own methodology for providing religious education to children with special needs.

Other Resources for Children with Special Needs

Adaptive First Eucharist Preparation Kit
3580-1 | $59.99

Adaptive Reconciliation Kit
3757-7 | $59.99

Adaptive Confirmation Preparation Kit
3877-2 | $59.99

Faith, Family and Children with Special Needs
David Rizzo
3651-8 | $12.95 | Paperback